Praise for *This Much I Know about Love Over Fear*

At a time when so many books on school leadership are written by people who have fled the classroom, who no longer stalk the corridors or dread wet lunchtimes, here's a book that oozes authenticity. John Tomsett reminds us of why great teaching matters so much and why great school leadership has to be built on classroom credibility. It's a book that is wise, funny, often deeply moving. It has taught me a lot – not least about myself, my own teaching and my leadership. Recommended.

Geoff Barton, head teacher, King Edward VI School

John Tomsett is a very rare kind of head teacher, and it's no surprise he's written a book that's equally rare, in that it is a book written by someone currently within the education system, about the education system, that is both apposite and well written. He writes with conviction and experience, both of which are necessary to say anything useful in a crowded field of books that are anodyne, vacuous or thinly disguised polemics.

John Tomsett the teacher comes through in every page; someone who still teachers, when many heads do not, and best of all still loves it. Loves it enough to still do it, to think about it, to write about it. It's often said that everyone has a book within them; sadly it's often not a good book, but this is a very good book indeed. Nothing can replace the experience of being in command, but a close second for anyone interested in accessing John's decades of wisdom, is to read about it here. Broad ranging yet still specific enough to burst with utility, if every head teacher were to read this, that wouldn't be a bad thing at all. And if anyone else in education were to read it too, that wouldn't be bad either. His school is a case study in putting your money where your mouth is, and I wish we had more people like him wherever children need an education.

Tom Bennett, founder of researchED, teacher, and columnist for the *TES*

I've rated John Tomsett as a head teacher and a commentator on education for some years now, so I had high expectations when I sat down to read this book. I have to say it exceeded them. It's full of the characteristic warmth, wit and wisdom readers of John's 'This much I know …' blog will already be familiar with.

Through autobiographical vignettes John shows clearly where his strong sense of moral purpose, as a school leader and as a human being, is grounded. He then moves to the educational focus of each chapter, and concludes with practical 'This much I know about …' bullet-point advice.

I found the book readable, refreshing and uplifting. John's conviction that improving the quality of teaching (and not simply focusing on the performance of teachers) should be the key focus of leadership is based on his experience and his personal knowledge informed by his extensive reading. It has much to offer teachers, and leaders at all levels, and it allows a fascinating insight into how this remarkable leader was formed, and subsequently developed. John lives the values he espouses.

So I'm sorry the professional golfing career didn't work out, John.

But I'm not, really ….

Jill Berry, education consultant, former head teacher

What a stroke of luck that John Tomsett never quite realised his dream to be a golf professional or a full-time sports journalist, but became a teacher instead. His success in the classroom and in running a school is not measured just by the fortunate pupils and colleagues who have worked with and learned from John. His influence is much wider. His 'This much I know …' blogs and ubiquitous presence on social media, his brilliant moving and inspirational talks are spell binding. In short order he has become a national educational phenomenon, with his roots firmly in the rich soil of the classroom, staffroom and school.

His debut book shows why. Beautifully written; John, as you'd expect of an outstanding teacher, is a great story-teller, thinks aloud and in the process causes others to think too.

A unique educational autobiography, it will rank alongside those of the likes of John Holt, Ted Sizer and Paulo Freire, as one you'll know exactly where it is on your bookshelf. You'll keep going back – a must read for all teachers, for the staff library and for future leaders, as well as for any post sixteen students who should consider teaching as still the best career to have.

Sir Tim Brighouse, former London schools commissioner and chief education officer for Birmingham and Oxfordshire

I loved this book. It is eclectic, human, very moving at times and filled with wisdom, knowledge and care. It combines biography, the distillation of experience and a wide canvas of research – a book for the head and the heart. John Tomsett has become a very important voice in education in Britain and this book shows why. He has great experience, knowledge and wisdom, all of which he shares, but it is the passion that will keep me coming back to it. This much I know about reading John Tomsett's book – I am unlikely to read a better education book this year.

David Cameron, The Real David Cameron Ltd

How could you not love this man? John Tomsett's book is a personal account of his own learning, modestly declaring 'This much I know about love over fear', drawing on his own experience, his family, his childhood, his teaching, his leadership, his poetry – and his golf. Through it all his values shine with the heat of a blast-furnace: 'respect, honesty and kindness'. Fear plays a minor role in this story; love overwhelms it.

Tomsett shows that love can be tough love. He may be nurturing and supportive as a head, but he is also demanding. However good a teacher you are, you need to be even better. He gives specific examples to illustrate how students can be taught to plan and write better essays, how seeing the head teacher engage a tough group of disengaged boys changed the culture in his school, how metaphors can be used to explain key concepts like 'film genre theory', how performance management can be performance development.

Some of the research Tomsett cites is a bit cherry-picked for my taste, and some of it treated a bit uncritically: not all research really proves what it claims, you can usually find some research to back up any belief, and some research findings can be interpreted to support conclusions that are not really what was found. But I am a pedantic research nerd and his overall message is sound. More important, it is presented in a way that will connect with teachers and bring to life the research and its applications to their practice.

When you work in education it is easy to get depressed and frustrated about things. Teaching is such a hard job; even doing it badly is demanding, but trying to do it well is an unending Herculean trial. Seeing – and sharing – the challenges that some young people face, and daily having to live with your impotence to remove them, can be profoundly draining. Interference from government, from inspectors, and from others with power and the desire to improve things, even if it is well-meant, rarely feels helpful. This book is an antidote to all that negativity. It is uplifting, affirming, passionate and deeply moving. It is about love, but not much about fear.

Robert Coe, professor of education, Durham University

John's honesty and refreshing approach separates this book from the plethora of dry, technical and anodyne texts on school improvement and frankly, makes *This Much I Know about Love Over Fear* special. John sets out the case that education can't be reduced to a technocratic painting-by-numbers process where we devise ever more sophisticated measures to ensure compliance to the method. John reminds us that teaching and leading teaching is all about relationships and the way we use what we know, let's call it wisdom, to inform and improve our work. The value of evidence and the implications of nailing your colours to the mast of an evidence-informed profession are carefully considered and resolved as John presents a compelling case for schools to harness research on their terms and as the servant of their needs. Evidence on tap not on top, to coin a phrase. John's wonderful stories about his childhood, the fateful round of golf at Liphook, his sonnet for the school caretaker tell us something about the man and his values and motivations that drive his work. John's passion for education and the way it has changed the circumstances of his own life is used to demonstrate the importance of the profession we share and our collective responsibility to challenge poor teaching and build a culture of continual improvement.

Kevan Collins, educationalist

From sixth-form dropout to inspiring head teacher, John Tomsett takes us on a personal journey, written with warmth and love – for his parents, his family, teachers and children. Readers of his blog will already know John as a very good writer who is widely read and educationally wise and this book benefits from its focus on teaching and the leadership of teaching as the top priorities for school leaders. Full of common sense, *This Much I Know about Love Over Fear* will help to improve your teaching, your school leadership and, just possibly, your golf handicap too.

Sir John Dunford, chair, Whole Education

This book surprised me. I know John-the-leader but *This Much I Know about Love Over Fear* is definitely written by John-the-teacher. Whether you are an NQT or have been a head teacher for years you must read this book. It will inspire you, challenge you and make you smile. John is the template for the 21st century head teacher that I aspire to be – *This Much I Know about Love Over Fear* should be on every teacher's wish list.

Vic Goddard, Passmores Academy

An inspiring read, which explores with great insight how strong leadership and quality teaching is the key to school achievement. John Tomsett is both practitioner and polemicist – and this fine book is a welcome and significant contribution to our increasingly urgent debate about raising standards and developing character amongst British school children.

Tristram Hunt, Labour MP

This much I know about John Tomsett: he writes beautifully. He thinks deeply. He brings to thinking and writing about teaching a powerful mix of autobiography, commitment and the deepest professional expertise. There is wisdom on every page of this book, and a genuinely insightful understanding of what it takes, really, to improve teaching, teachers and schools. This much I learn from John Tomsett: that the quality of schooling depends on the quality of relationships which schools can sustain. Read this book.

Professor Chris Husbands, director, UCL Institute of Education

What happens when we tell stories as leaders? Our values get exposed as part of the narrative, and people lean in and listen. In his deeply engaging *This Much I Know about Love Over Fear* John Tomsett allows us to see his humanity, to connect with his passion for young people, and to share the learning from his creative, relational style of leadership.

Frequent vignettes point to the value John places on engaging students in the classroom, '... time when I could influence what they did and how they thought', and it's clear that he sees his role as leader of teachers in the same way: *This Much I Know about Love Over Fear* is what adults and children alike need to flourish. John takes wisdom he's developed from a lifetime of mishaps and breakthroughs (including 12 years of headship), aligns it beautifully with his wide reading of education and leadership literature, and offers practical insights and helpful suggestions in his humble 'This much I know' lists.

If you want to reconnect with your moral purpose in teaching; if you want gritty and honest ideas for transformative school leadership; if you thirst for provocation that will keep you always striving to be better than you were yesterday, this book will delight and help in equal measure.

Ruth Kennedy, founder director, ThePublicOffice, school governor, former teacher

At a time when much of our school system is being driven by the various elements of high-stakes accountability – graded observations, performance management, league tables and a punitive inspection system – John not only highlights the folly of this approach but, crucially, he articulates with great clarity an alternative. Drawing on his personal and professional experience he argues that we need to remove fear from the system, develop cultures that focus on the learning of leaders, teachers and pupils and create schools which are exciting, challenging and supportive places to work and learn.

Sir Alasdair Macdonald, former head teacher of Morpeth School

This Much I Know about Love Over Fear was not what I had expected – an unusual twist on leadership, in a way that feels fresh and provides a new slant on the concept. It's a book you should be advised to sit and read cover to cover, and then to take the time to re-read. There is a plethora of good advice, far too much to absorb in one sitting. I'll be going back, dipping in to chapters to find the advice I need at the right time. It made me realise that times haven't changed, kids haven't changed. It is so overwhelming, positive and uplifting, the tale of a wonderful life intertwined with rich experiences of leadership. Beautiful.

Dr Rona Mackenzie, principal, Lincoln UTC

Part autobiography, part practical guide, you will not find a more heartfelt and honest account of what really matters for teaching and learning. For anyone who cares about the future of our children this is a compelling and hugely enjoyable read from one of our most respected school leaders.

Dr Lee Elliot Major, chief executive, The Sutton Trust,
co-author of the *Teaching and Learning Toolkit*

John Tomsett rightly sees himself as a head teacher. But he is also a thinker – about relationships, humanity, evidence and all that contributes to great teaching and a positive school culture. This is the new frontier for schools. We are lucky to have John and this wonderful book to guide us.

Fiona Millar, school governor and *Guardian* columnist

It isn't often that a book on education could be described as 'moving' but *This Much I Know about Love Over Fear* by John Tomsett is just that. As one of the nation's most successful school leaders, John both passes on some of the wisdom he has learned from his years in teaching and combines it with a narrative about his life and his family.

His commitment to the moral purpose of education shines through. His gratitude for the role education played in his own life is reflected in his uncompromising belief that nothing should get in the way of providing the same life changing opportunity for today's generation of young people.

The book a testament to the importance of good teachers and contains a wealth of good advice about how to do the job. It is a pleasure to read and a source of invaluable advice.

Estelle Morris, former secretary of state for education

You know the sort of book that, as you read it, it meets you halfway. You recognise many of your own ideas, values, hopes and mistakes. Well this book was it, for me. John Tomsett nails it. Everything he writes is focused on the core business: great teaching, great provision for every student. 'Make sure your school leadership team is focused upon the core business of school, improving teaching and learning.'

I'm a skimmer. I get through a lot of text. Fast. I can't remember the last professional book I read where I didn't skip or skim a page. I didn't skip a sentence of *This Much I Know about Love Over Fear*. It's a compelling read and beautifully written. It embraces John's philosophy of education, autobiography, wider management theories and a sensible commentary on what it looks like in his school. Absolutely tremendous.

It's a tough call to include significant moments of personal history. But John does this from a deep well and respect for his parents and the community where he grew up. Without ever becoming sentimental he describes the influence of both parents: his mother's stoicism and his father's love of the natural world and his incredible work ethic. He weaves aspects of his own story into each chapter. And some of it is hilarious. The firework fiasco. You will have to buy the book to find out what happened.

John's thoughts on the primacy of the quality of relationships with students apply equally to his colleagues. And he draws on ancient wisdom and recent research to back this up – Fullan, Elder, EEF, Nuttall, Seneca and Virgil. Of course he knows this already, but very good to have his observations grounded in a wider pool of research.

It's a big ask: to write a serious book about the principles and practicalities of leadership. John's book is accessible, thoughtful, moving and funny in equal measure. I predict *This Much I Know about Love Over Fear* will be essential reading for every leader of learning, from head teacher to NQT, in every school.

Mary Myatt, adviser and inspector http://marymyatt.com

I am uniquely placed to review John Tomsett's book – I work in his school! Happily, the book captures the best of John's leadership: it conveys his passion for education, his commitment and care for those he leads, and it captures his leadership wisdom.

At a time of much fear, when most head teachers are being driven to distraction, with too many prospective heads avoiding the role altogether, John provides the ballast of hope and guidance. The book is full of deftly crafted personal stories that touch the heart, woven together with useful professional insights borne of much experience. It makes for a book that is quite unique and well worth reading. Oh, and if you are wondering – he is a great boss to work for!

Alex Quigley, director of learning and research, Huntington School

The title of this book does it a disservice – it should be just one word: Love, for this is a love story. It is imbued with love for family, for friends, for teachers, for pupils, for colleagues, for literature, poetry and prose, for music, for sport, for thought, and most of all for the art of teaching and learning. A deeply humane book that gives some excellent insights into the how of education and leadership. I am sure the words of wisdom contained in this book will be a thoughtful and supportive companion for many a successful career.

Martin Robinson, author *Trivium 21c*

If evidence-based practice is about 'integrating the best available research evidence with professional expertise' then John's book suggests he is a master of both.

Dr Jonathan Sharples, Education Endowment Foundation

For me, John Tomsett represents the soul of education, always keeping what matters most at the centre of everything he says and does: great teaching and moral purpose. *This Much I Know about Love Over Fear* captures that spirit perfectly: personal history, golf, poetry and educational wisdom grounded in experience combine beautifully to create a book that is both practical and profound.

Tom Sherrington, head teacher, Highbury Grove School

This is a funny, warm, and touching book but it is also grounded in practical thoughts and ideas for how to run a school. It mixes anecdotes and autobiography with educational research and John's own experiences as a head to set out a series of clear statements on education. The best thing about the book is how John's voice and personality shines out from every chapter. By the end it's as if you've worked in his school for years, and you feel comforted, challenged and enthused by that.

Jonathan Simons, head of education, Policy Exchange

John Tomsett is an inspirational teacher, head teacher and leader. In sharing his wisdom in this wonderful book he inspires, educates and, occasionally, even brings a lump to the throat. John has a wonderful way of telling stories in a very human way, explaining his deep thinking with humility and bringing the book to life with real examples and practical advice.

David Weston, chief executive, Teacher Development Trust

THIS MUCH I KNOW
about LOVE OVER FEAR ...
CREATING A CULTURE FOR TRULY GREAT TEACHING

JOHN TOMSETT

Crown House Publishing Limited
www.crownhouse.co.uk

First published by
Crown House Publishing Limited
Crown Buildings, Bancyfelin, Carmarthen, Wales, SA33 5ND, UK
www.crownhouse.co.uk

and

Crown House Publishing Company LLC
6 Trowbridge Drive, Suite 5, Bethel, CT 06801, USA
www.crownhousepublishing.com

First published 2015. Reprinted 2015.

The cover image is used with permission of The Press, York and Ross Hardman. The comment on
page 23 is reproduced with permission of eNotes. The extracts on page 28, page 29 and page 155
are used with permission of Alex Quigley. The image on page 38 is © goodluz, fotolia.com.
The list on page 96 is copyright © 2004 by John Wiley & Sons, Inc. All rights reserved. It is used
with permission of Wiley. The interview on pages 150 –155 is used with permission of David
Lamb. The tweet on page 168 is used with permission of Tom Bennett. The figure on page 172
is used with permission of Kevan Collins.

Quotes from Ofsted documents used in this publication have been approved under an
Open Government Licence. Please visit www.nationalarchives.gov.uk/open-government-
licence/version/3/.

British Library Cataloguing-in-Publication Data

A catalogue entry for this book is available from the British Library.

Print ISBN: 978-184590982-6
Mobi ISBN: 978-184590983-3
ePub ISBN: 978-184590984-0
ePDF ISBN: 978-184590985-7

LCCN 2015940767
Printed and bound in the UK by
Gomer Press, Llandysul, Ceredigion

In grateful memory of my dad
Ernest Harry Tomsett
(1927–1985)

It hardly mattered to him that the book was forgotten and that it served no use; and the question of its worth at any time seemed trivial. He did not have the illusion that he would find himself there, in that fading print; and yet, he knew, a small part of him that he could not deny was there, and would be there.

John Williams, *Stoner*

Gratitudes

I owe two special thank yous. Firstly to Caroline Lenton at Crown House Publishing who, when she identified its structure, persuaded me to finish this book when it would have been far easier to have abandoned it completely. And secondly, to Louise, Joe and Olly for putting up with me for so long.

The list of other people I need to thank – and it's a long list – is covered, I think, by my final line of the book.

Contents

A family portrait

He had left school at 14 to become a messenger boy, the prelude to becoming a lifelong postman. He could read but rarely wrote. He excelled at gardening and golf. She had fallen ill when just 13 and never completed her formal education. She resorted to being a cleaner and read voraciously to nurture her intellect. She 'did' for Mrs Wilkins in the village, keeping her baby with her in the pram whilst she cleaned. The portrait was her idea.

He had finished his post round by mid-morning and the noon appointment at the photographer's gave him time to get back to the sorting office by early afternoon. He had taken his wedding suit to work, changing out of his uniform in the restroom. He combed his Brylcreemed hair back just before the flashbulb popped. He was approaching his thirty-first birthday.

That Monday she had caught the number 119 bus with their daughter to travel the two miles into town. She wore her best yellow polka-dot number and dressed her daughter in pink. All their clothes had been bought on the never-never from the catalogue; *four shillings a week for thirty-six weeks*. She was 22 years old.

⁓‿⌓

The image is one of celebration and aspiration. It celebrates the family unit. Their hands reveal a great deal: one of his linked with his daughter's and the other on his wife's shoulder in protective embrace; her hand is ostentatiously spread upon the arm of the chair displaying her wedding ring. They aspired to be more than their lot; the professional portrait with their firstborn must have felt like a middle-class extravagance. They could have been film stars. Burton and Taylor.

So, not a qualification between them, but both knew there was something more to life than low-paid jobs and living in a council house. Their indomitable spirit – a sense that values drive us, that honest graft is respectable, that life is there to be seized – resonates in this image. They are staring straight out of the picture and into the future. It was September 1958 and they look like nothing could stop them.

And these were my parents.

Why this book?

Choice

> In every single sphere of British influence, the upper echelons of power in 2013 are held overwhelmingly by the privately educated or the affluent middle class. To me, from my background, I find that truly shocking.
>
> Sir John Major

The Monty Python team's 'Four Yorkshiremen' makes any account of a 1970s council house childhood open to ridicule.[1] The sketch sees four wealthy Yorkshiremen trying to outdo each other's working-class credentials: 'Well, of course, we had it tough. We used to 'ave to get up out of shoebox at twelve o'clock at night and lick road clean wit' tongue.'

The parody, like all good parodies, is rooted in a certain truth. It also makes me hesitant to recount what I remember of growing up. But the truth of my childhood has shaped my life; my council-house foundations still influence my decision-making today, forty years on. To understand why I hold my core beliefs you need to know a bit more about my upbringing in deepest East Sussex in the 1970s.

I have four siblings. Seven of us lived in a three-bedroomed council house. I shared a bedroom with my two brothers, David and Ian, and my sisters, Bev and Heather, shared another. The house had an outside toilet and we had a wee bucket in the corner of our bedroom if we needed it during the night. Occasionally one of us would stumble around in the dark and knock it over; its contents would leak through the floorboards and a couple of the white polystyrene tiles on the living room ceiling below would have taken on a sepia tone by breakfast time.

In 1970, the household family income was little more than £10 a week. Dad grew vegetables and we had three fruit trees at the far end of the

---

[1] *At Last the 1948 Show*, ITV (1967). Available at: https://www.youtube.com/watch?v=VKHFZBUTA4k.

garden; sometimes he would come home with a pheasant he had killed in his van on his post round. Despite dad's attempts at the good life, mother often had to buy our food on tick at the village store until dad was paid on the Friday. It took just one extra loaf a week for her to be overspent.

Our clothes came from jumble sales. I often didn't have any shorts and had to wear my school trousers rolled up to the knee for PE, something which feels marginally humiliating even now. Mother knitted us jumpers endlessly – something she still does, on occasion, for our sons. We all wore second-hand school uniforms.

The house was surrounded by a huge field which sloped down to a stream. We would spend every waking moment in the summer outside, catching trout, making hay-bale igloos, creating our own entertainment.

We holidayed at home, having days out in the summer to places like Norman's Bay near Eastbourne. We could have invented the concept of a staycation. If we were lucky we were lent a car by dad's friend who owned a garage in the village. We once spent a week in Crofton, a mining town just outside Wakefield, with family friends. Another time we went to Scotland and stayed with my auntie. Seven of us in an Opel Rekord; I crouched the ten hours and 400 miles to the Scottish borders in the back near-side footwell. I first went abroad when I was at university.

As kids we didn't really know how relatively poor we were but my mother did. I can see her standing at the kitchen sink with her hands in the basin staring out of the window and repeating aloud her favourite mantra, 'God give me strength to bear that which I cannot change.' In some ways mother's mantra has proven to be a motivating force for me.

I hope it's easier, having read this brief account of my childhood, to understand my sense of moral purpose as a school leader, my foundations. A good education allows you to choose your path in life, and I don't want one single student of mine to ever wonder what they've missed because they haven't had a choice.

This much I know for sure

Write what you know. That should leave you with a lot of free time.

Howard Nemerov

I teach a theory of knowledge course and we spend hours discussing how we know what we know. The more we talk, the less I think I know. Like most people who have lived beyond their youth, my certainties about life have dissolved away as the years have passed. And yet experience counts. Having taught for over a quarter of a century and led schools for well over a decade, I have a good idea of what it takes to be a decent enough English state school head teacher.

Whilst I've always had a propensity to write, I haven't always been sure that I've anything so valuable to say that people will bother reading what I've written. That changed to some extent in June 2012 when I began my blog where I ruminate on what I have learnt about education – and occasionally life – over the fifty years I've lived on this planet.

Without me realising it, my blog began when I was asked to talk to a small group of deputy heads about what it's like to be a head teacher. I rejected the idea of delivering yet another PowerPoint presentation; few have any power and most have little point. Instead I bullet-pointed a dozen things I knew about being a head teacher.

When I walked into the room, the previous presenter was finishing his PowerPoint with a three-minute video of why his school is so great. The deputies were palpably relieved when I shoved all the tables together and distributed my one side of A4 and just talked.

Back in April 2012, having been a head teacher for nine years, at the age of 47, this much I knew …

- I hardly remember a single lesson from my own school days. In third year French, I fell off my seat backwards and Mr P made me lie on the floor for the rest of the lesson. Anyone who says teaching is getting worse has a short memory – much of the profession in the 1970s was shocking!

- You need to know your core purpose – what it is that gets you out of bed each day to come to work. At Huntington School, ours is 'to inspire confident learners who will thrive in a changing world', and that guides every difficult decision we make. It certainly helps me if I need to challenge inadequate teaching. And what you must do is restructure your school to accommodate your core purpose, not contort your core purpose around the existing structures.

- Education is about relationships. Michael Fullan is great on this: you have to develop the culture of the school, and every interaction you have as a leader with students and staff helps set the tone of the place. That is why the values system of your school matters so much.

- Our values are respect, honesty and kindness. When I came to Huntington, one sixth-former said to me, 'You don't enjoy main school, you just get through it – and if you cause trouble they nail you.' Through four-and-a-half years of relentlessly demonstrating behaviours which reflect our values, the school is now a pleasant place and the results have never been better.

- I understand what Wilshaw and Gove are on about when they say context is irrelevant. But whilst the fact that some of my students will have heard several thousand fewer words by the age of 3 than my son did at that age is not an excuse for my students' limited literacy, it does help to explain why they find it more difficult to read and write.

- The coalition's educational emphasis is encapsulated in the fact that they equate the BTEC First Diploma in construction, where students learn the basics of brick-laying, painting and decorating, plumbing, electrical wiring and plastering, with Grade 6 in the flute.

- Without being idealistically naive, stick to what you believe in rather than be a feather for each educational wind that blows – there are some things in education which are eternal verities.

- I have to create the conditions for students and staff to thrive; if I can do that, then we will all grow – students, staff, parents and governors.

- Target your resources on what matters most and just make do with everything else. Teaching is the thing that makes most difference to children's academic performance so invest in high quality continuing professional development (CPD) – train people to be good teachers. Find a way to do catering and cleaning as cheaply as possible and then invest in your staff.

- When I admitted I couldn't be a perfect head teacher, I became better at my job. It was in my fourth year as a head and I have prioritised ruthlessly ever since. Some things can slip through my fingers now and then but I still sort out the important stuff.

- Keep things simple. If I ever write a book about headship, I'll call it 'The Power of Simplicity'.

- To some extent, I missed my eldest son growing up. Joe is 15 years old now and a young man. When I cuddle him I can't believe the width of his shoulders and he squirms away as quick as he can. He thinks I'm an idiot! Read *Death of a Salesman* if you want to know why you should spend more time with the people you love. I taught it last year and now, whenever my sons ask me to do something, I do it, irrespective of my work.

So, that's how writing about headship began for me. I set up a blog and posted my first offering under the title, 'This Much I Know (With Apologies to the Observer Magazine)'. My first 'This Much I Know' proved popular so I continued to post on my blog, reflecting further upon leading schools and the core business of schools – teaching and learning.

Writing my blog clarifies my thinking. I have lots of material in my head about work, like bits of space debris; blogging melds them into the satellite which directs my personal satnav. The key thing about what I write, and especially about this book, is that it is largely based on my experience. It is my personal knowledge – I know it through experience. But I also read a great deal of literature about leadership in education and this helps me to process what I experience. What I have come to know has been tested daily over twelve years of headship.

It is this combination of experience, knowledge and other people's expert research that I have drawn on to write this book, and which I am writing at a time when there is a huge fork in the road for head teachers: one route leads to executive headship across a number of schools and the other takes head teachers back into the classroom to be the head *teacher*.

As a head teacher I have always taught. I cannot imagine a life without teaching. Teaching is still the best part of my day, bar none. My strongly held belief is that if the head teacher is not teaching, or engaged in helping others to improve their teaching, in his school, then he is missing the point. The only thing head teachers need obsess themselves with is improving the quality of teaching, both their colleagues' and their own.

What follows is designed to be of practical use for school leaders. It's pretty short. It's deliberately designed to be an easy read. Each chapter begins with a short autobiographical vignette which prefaces the educational heart of the chapter, all topped off with a 'This Much I Know' style bullet-point list.

Creating a truly great school takes patience. Ultimately, truly great schools don't suddenly exist. You grow great teachers first, who, in turn, grow a truly great school. A truly great school grows like an oak tree over years, not overnight like a mushroom.

And to grow a truly great school love has to triumph over fear – this much I know for sure.

Chapter 1

Truly great teaching

My first teacher

A garden is a grand teacher. It teaches patience and careful watchfulness; it teaches industry and thrift; above all it teaches entire trust.

Gertrude Jekyll

When I began my teaching career at Eastbourne Sixth Form College one of my biggest influences was Kate Darwin. We were appointed on the same day but she was nearly twenty years older than me. Kate is a truly great teacher and one of the wisest people I know.

We shared the driving from Brighton to Eastbourne and within the confines of our cars we swapped stories. Kate's dad had been to Cambridge and won a university prize which her husband-to-be, Chris, was awarded a generation later. Kate's dad was a head teacher. He died suddenly when Kate was only 18 years old. He had written with the same ink pen for the whole of his life; the story of her dad and his Waterman is best told in a sonnet I wrote for Kate:

Different Strokes

His choice of pen remained the same
From undergraduate Cambridge days
To signing his headmaster's name –
A Waterman in mottled beige.
The cursive blacksmith's art had honed
The ink-filled gold into a tool
For use by him and him alone –
His hand made them inseparable.

Gold outlasts all. The pen was left
A legacy, bequeathed to her

Whose writing pleased the family most:
But straining through the unknown curves
It snapped, to leave the nib's new host
Mourning afresh, doubly bereft.

And whilst not educated like Kate's father, my dad was a teacher in many ways too. Apart from learning how to play golf with him, he taught me a lot about the countryside. He'd grown up four miles from his school and had to walk there and back every day through the Sussex fields. He taught me how to strip a sapling for a bow and arrow, how to predict the weather, how to catch a fish. I can remember as a 6-year-old watching him stalk a trout in an eddied pool on a Sussex stream for nearly an hour before he caught it. He was a study in patient persistence.

I hadn't realised quite what a teacher he was until my eldest sister, Bev, who knew him that much longer than I did, wrote to me nearly thirty years after he'd died:

> Dad was always there for each of us as we grew up. He took Dave [my eldest brother] and me for long walks in the country and knew everything about nature. He helped me with my stoolball, helped me ice and decorate my Xmas cake, and even tried to teach me how to hit a golf ball!
>
> Luckily for all of us his job did not interfere with home life. Once he clocked off he'd finished until the alarm went off the next morning. He was able to enjoy his post round out in the countryside, and was a valuable member of that community. He helped feed the lambs at the farm, took an old lady flowers and eggs, posted her letters and was the only human contact that she had.
>
> Every March he would pick the first primroses of the year and send them to Auntie Nancy. He was out in the fresh air every day, observing all four seasons, not confined to four brick walls like the majority of us are.
>
> I see dad in his own way as a teacher. He was not well-educated – through no fault of his own – but he taught us right from wrong. He showed us how to respect the countryside, kindness,

honesty, stoicism, love and gratitude. Above all he was able to give each of us his time, a gift more precious than status or money. He was a very wise man.

After I'd wiped the tears away, one thing that struck me about Bev's words was the first three things she cites which dad showed us: *how to respect the countryside, kindness* and *honesty*. They are the exact same values of our school: respect, honesty and kindness.

Dad tended roses with pure artistry. He died three years from retirement and the chance to lie in his own bed of roses forever. And just as Kate was chosen to receive her dad's pen, I became the depository for all my dad's possessions. Mother still sends me odd artefacts she finds, like his National Service discharge documents – he was conscripted into the navy for two years.

His glasses were a shock when I opened the case; they are half-rimmed ones and the way he used to look over the top of them and grin seemed encased with them. Mother sent me this letter which is now framed on my office wall:

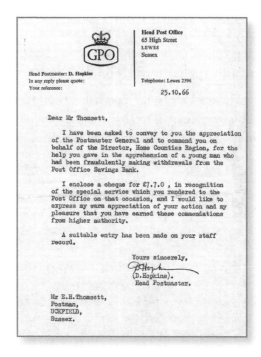

In the event of a fire this is the first thing I would grab. The letter captures perfectly dad's honesty which Bev had so sharply observed, and I love the way the class system – which pervaded mid-1960s Britain – is clearly evident in the letter's tone. Worth noting too that in 1966, £7.7.0 was a week's wages to a postie.

Truly great teaching

> The fundamental purpose of school is learning, not teaching.
>
> Richard DuFour

Before we go any further, it's important to explore the core business of any school: teaching. And it's worth emphasising that we are trying to focus upon teaching not teachers. Professor Chris Husbands explained beautifully why it is worth making this subtle distinction in a blog post where he pointed out, 'We can all teach well and we can all teach badly … more generally, we can all teach better: teaching changes and develops. Skills improve. Ideas change. Practice alters. It's teaching, not teachers.' [1] This is a helpful distinction because it depersonalises pedagogy so that we can at least begin to talk about improving teaching without being critical of the individual person who is doing the teaching – something which is generally so hard to achieve.

The more I read about teaching, the more difficult it is to define teaching, let alone truly great teaching. If you read Graham Nuthall's *The Hidden Lives of Learners*,[2] or Daniel Willingham's *Why Don't Students Like School?*[3]

---

[1] Chris Husbands, Great Teachers or Great Teaching? Why McKinsey Got It Wrong, *IOE London Blog* (10 October 2013). Available at: https://ioelondonblog.wordpress.com/2013/10/10/great-teachers-or-great-teaching-why-mckinsey-got-it-wrong/.

[2] Graham Nuthall, *The Hidden Lives of Learners* (Wellington: New Zealand Council for Educational Research Press, 2007).

[3] Daniel Willingham, *Why Don't Students Like School? A Cognitive Scientist Answers Questions About How the Mind Works and What It Means for the Classroom* (San Francisco, CA: Jossey-Bass, 2010).

or Paul Hirst's 'What is Teaching?',[4] you'll understand why anyone could feel confused about what truly great teaching looks and sounds like.

Hirst says, 'Successful teaching would seem to be simply teaching which does in fact bring about the desired learning.'[5] Within that seemingly simple statement lies the complex relationship between teacher and student, something quite delicate but crucial to successful teaching and learning. And when Biesta writes, 'it is not within the power of the teacher to give this gift [of teaching], but depends on the fragile interplay between the teacher and the student. Teachers can at most try and hope, but they cannot force the gift [of teaching] upon their students,'[6] what he is hinting at is the primacy of teacher–student relationships. Because teaching is a human activity, the relationship between teacher and student is fundamental to whether the student learns from the teaching.

With Hirst and Biesta in mind, I think those best qualified to define the qualities of a successful teacher – and so give us a good idea of what constitutes successful teaching – are our students.

One of the most constructive organisations I have worked with as a head teacher is John Corrigan's Group 8 Education. John is an excellent coach and he articulated very clearly a way for us to talk about teaching with our students. One of the activities we undertook was based upon John Corrigan's work on what students look for in a successful teacher.[7] Our work with Group 8 centred on thirty descriptors about teachers and teaching which had been shaped by John and his team over several years.

---

[4] Paul H. Hirst, What is Teaching?, in *Knowledge and the Curriculum: A Collection of Philosophical Papers* (London: Routledge and Kegan Paul, 1974).

[5] Hirst, What is Teaching?

[6] Gert J. J. Biesta, Giving Teaching Back to Education: Responding to the Disappearance of the Teacher, *Phenomenology & Practice* 6(2) (2012): 35–49. Available at: https://ejournals.library.ualberta.ca/index.php/pandpr/article/viewFile/19860/15386.

[7] See http://gr8education.com and John Corrigan, Improving Student Learning Outcomes in the 21st Century: White Paper (Group 8 Education). Available at: http://gr8education.com/discussion-paper/.

In rank order of importance to students, these are the common features of good teaching identified by our students from the bank of thirty descriptors:

1 Teachers respect me.

2 Teachers are knowledgeable in their subject.

3 Teachers are friendly, approachable and willing to listen.

4 Teachers are positive, enthusiastic and have a sense of humour.

5 Teachers encourage and help me to succeed.

6 In class I do work that is interesting and challenging for me.

7 Teachers celebrate my progress and achievements.

8 Teachers remind me that my success depends on my effort.

9 My classes have clear rules for how I should behave throughout the class.

10 Teachers provide me with useful feedback on my work.

It's a pretty good set of descriptors, one forged and selected by students – the only ones who have experienced the full range of teacher quality. This list of the characteristics of good teachers, as hierarchically selected by our own students, only confirmed my thinking about the best teachers I have known. I would suggest that any group of students, when asked for the five key features of a good teacher, will always give you essentially the same answer, namely that good teachers:

1 Respect us as adults.

2 Are enthusiastic.

3 Make lessons interesting.

4 Know their subject.

5 Explain things clearly and help if we don't understand.

So much of this feedback from students about teachers returns us to relationships. Number one for students in an idealised teacher is that the teacher respects them. At Huntington we adopt the mantra, 'Always be the adult in the situation', based on the principle of unconditional positive regard as espoused by Carl Rogers.[8] Furthermore, one of our three core values is respect, and we have always included in our school development plan the aspiration to work in a school where people acknowledge the fallibility of the human condition. We all get things wrong; we just have to try hard not to make the same mistake twice!

So, if we can get the relationship between teacher and student right, we might just be able to encourage the students to accept Biesta's gift of successful teaching. Veronica Weusten's *The Talented Teacher* is a little known gem of a publication in which the author outlines her view that successful teaching depends upon a teacher's character.[9] I would implore any teacher, youthful or experienced, to read and reflect upon it.

Weusten's book is about the importance of personal authenticity in teaching. She says, in an echo of Biesta, that whilst you may want to be a skilled teacher, it is your pupils who will determine whether or not you in fact are one because, ultimately, pupils prefer teachers they like. Her list of the characteristics a teacher should have, according to students, is remarkably similar to mine: '[a successful teacher] has humour, is pleasant, and maintains classroom order and structure … is able to explain well, is patient and is just'.[10]

So, according to our own students and Weusten, good classroom relationships are key to effective teaching. However, an effective learning environment is not enough to determine or guarantee good teaching because, as Hirst so clearly points out, good teaching depends upon students learning what you think you've taught them. Every teacher in the land has taught a great lesson but discovered at some point, either

---

[8] See Jerold Bozarth, *Rogers' Therapeutic Conditions: Evolution Theory and Practice. Vol. 3: Unconditional Positive Regard* (Monmouth: PCCS Books, 2001).

[9] Veronica Weusten, *The Talented Teacher* [Weusten en Hoornstra], 11th edn (2013). Available to purchase at: http://www.degeliefdeleraar.nl/en/webwinkel/de-geliefde-leraar/.

[10] Weusten, *The Talented Teacher.*

near the end of the lesson or at the beginning of the next one, that what she had thought she'd taught them had not been learnt by the students.

In my first year of teaching I spent hours and hours marking students' work. At the end of the year I sat down with each one of my students and reflected upon his or her progress. I must have written 'Do not paraphrase!' tens of times in the margins of Alison's essays over the year, yet she highlighted in one simple question the ineffectiveness of my teaching when she asked, 'What does "paraphrase" mean?'

This experience with Alison reminded me of the old joke: there were two small boys, John and Jim, who were friends. Jim had a dog. One day they were taking the dog for a walk and Jim said proudly: 'I've taught the dog to whistle.' 'What do you mean?' said John. 'He's not whistling.' 'I know,' said Jim. 'But I said I'd taught him; I didn't say he'd learnt.'[11]

One of the highlights of my career has been working with Professor Rob Coe from the Centre for Evaluation and Monitoring at the University of Durham. In 2014 he co-authored a report for the Sutton Trust entitled, *What Makes Great Teaching?*[12] The report reviews over 200 pieces of research to identify the elements of teaching with the strongest evidence of improving attainment.

Coe and his co-authors conclude that great teaching is that which leads to improved student progress. They acknowledge the difficulty of pinning down exactly what constitutes great teaching, and their reflections on the matter are similar to Hirst's:

> We define effective teaching as that which leads to improved student achievement using outcomes that matter to their future success. Defining effective teaching is not easy. The research

---

[11] Paul Green-Armytage, Colour Zones: Connecting Colour Order and Everyday Language, in *9th Congress of the International Colour Association, Proceedings of SPIE*, Vol. 4421 (2002), pp. 976–979.

[12] Robert Coe, Cesare Aloisi, Steve Higgins and Lee Elliot Major, *What Makes Great Teaching?* (London: Sutton Trust, 2014).

keeps coming back to this critical point: student progress is the yardstick by which teacher quality should be assessed.[13]

It is hard to disagree with Coe and Hirst. In the end, what is the point of teaching if students do not make academic progress? What I like about the Sutton Trust report is the list of six common components suggested by research that teachers should consider when assessing teaching quality:

1 (Pedagogical) Content knowledge.

2 Quality of instruction.

3 Classroom climate.

4 Classroom management.

5 Teacher beliefs.

6 Professional behaviours.[14]

The authors explain that the third component, classroom climate, covers 'quality of interactions between teachers and students, and teacher expectations: the need to create a classroom that is constantly demanding more, but still recognising students' self-worth. It also involves attributing student success to effort rather than ability and valuing resilience to failure (grit).'[15]

All six components are important in helping to define great teaching, but I think classroom climate is a welcome inclusion as it acknowledges the importance of relationships as well as the value of resilience to failure, something I come back to in Chapter 11 on the growth mindset.

Whilst I might have established how darned hard it is to pin down what teaching is, one of the activities a school's teaching staff ought to undertake is to agree collaboratively on what it is they think constitutes

---

[13] Coe et al., *What Makes Great Teaching?*

[14] Coe et al., *What Makes Great Teaching?*

[15] Coe et al., *What Makes Great Teaching?*

truly great teaching. Until they agree what they think truly great teaching looks like, how can they aspire to be truly great teachers?

It doesn't really matter what the Teachers' Standards say or what the Ofsted criteria claim good teaching might look like, or even how, according to Professor Rob Coe, the existing evidence identifies great teaching: colleagues within the same school will profit from engaging in a discussion about what they mean when they talk about truly great teaching. Such a discussion is, logically, fundamental to our profession.

At Huntington we subscribe to Professor Rob Coe's view that great teaching is that which leads to improved student progress, but we have also thought hard about what we think good teaching and learning might look like. As a team of 125 teachers and teaching assistants, we agreed our own 'Features of Truly Great Teaching' and have now adopted them above the ever-changing Ofsted criteria. It may be easy for us to do since we were recently inspected, but Sir Michael Wilshaw made it clear in his 2012 speech to the RSA that there is no prescribed way to teach.[16]

This poster on page 19 can be found inside our teacher planners, and it is what we use when we are observing lessons as a support for post-observation developmental discussions.

The very process of engaging in the discussion which led to this set of criteria for truly great teaching was highly valuable in itself; importantly, we undertake a review of the descriptors every two years so that we involve new staff in the process of owning the definition of truly great teaching.

---

[16] Michael Wilshaw, What Is a Good Teacher? [video], *Royal Society of Arts* (3 April 2012). Available at: http://www.thersa.org/events/video/archive/what-is-a-good-teacher.

Truly Great Teaching at Huntington School

Teachers have **high expectations** of students. Lessons are appropriately **challenging** and risk taking; they foster curiosity and inspire **creative thinking**.

Assessment is used to progress learning. A **range of feedback strategies** is used which students act upon to make or exceed expected progress. DIRT is built into lessons.

Questioning is used to develop thinking. Open questions are planned to deepen understanding. Thinking time and oral rehearsal are built in.

Teachers know the students in front of them. We are flexible, and **the needs of different groups of students are planned for** so that they can all achieve great outcomes.

Teaching and Learning strategies are used to ensure that **teaching is engaging, relevant and purposeful.** Time is managed expertly, and progress is effectively reviewed. Students are well prepared for the demands of the new curriculum and are given chances to develop **memory retention.**

Behaviour for Learning is well managed so that students can move from 'compliant' to 'active' learners.

A **'Growth Mindset'** is encouraged in all students and staff. We aim to develop proficient and independent learners, who are intrinsically motivated by the reward of achievement. We are all part of a learning community.

Teachers **make a positive contribution to school life and live by the school's core values.** They demonstrate a range of personal qualities and skills: encouragement; humour; acute emotional intelligence; creativity; reflection; effective communication skills.

Teachers have **excellent subject knowledge.** Research is key to the development of pedagogy. Time is invested in researching current thinking and good practice.

High standards in **Literacy and Numeracy** are promoted by all teachers, and underpin learning in all subject areas.

Huntington School

This much I know about truly great teaching

- Truly great teaching is hard to define but it has to do with your students making tremendous progress.

- To be a truly great teacher you have to like the students before they like you – as Rita Pierson says, 'Kids don't learn from people they don't like.'[17]

- Truly great teaching requires a certain amount of gritty relentlessness.

- When students find it hard to learn, truly great teachers think of new ways of teaching to overcome the students' barriers to learning.

- I've seen truly great teachers talk to students for an hour without break and hold them in the metaphorical palm of their hand.

---

17 Rita Pierson, Every Kid Needs a Champion [video], *TED* (May 2013). Available at: http://www.ted.com/talks/rita_pierson_every_kid_needs_a_champion/transcript?language=en.

Chapter 2

You can always be that little bit better

Choosing to be better

> Don't bother just to be better than your contemporaries or predecessors. Try to be better than yourself.
>
> William Faulkner

One of the best players I ever played golf with was Paul Way. He was the superstar of the Sussex team in the late 1970s and early 1980s. He was supremely self-assured. Way worked hard at his golf game and had the most perfect swing. He won tournament after tournament as an amateur, culminating in him being crowned the English Amateur Stroke Play Champion in 1981.

In 1982, his first year as a professional golfer, Way won the KLM Dutch Open. The next year he qualified for the Ryder Cup and was paired with Severiano Ballesteros; he won three matches out of five against the Americans. He was a member of the victorious Ryder Cup team in 1985. In 1986 he won the European PGA championship. In 1987 he won the European Open. Tony Jacklin, the Ryder Cup captain, once said that Way could be 'as good as he wants to be'.

Way and I were members of the eight-man under 23 Sussex team to play Hampshire in 1981. I stood on the sixteenth fairway that summer morning and watched Way up on the green attempting a twenty-foot putt to win the hole in front of hundreds of onlookers. He hit the putt and walked after the ball, which inevitably dropped into the hole; he scooped the ball out of the hole with his putter as he strode by and, all in one movement, knocked it off the green. Oh, the elan of it all! The next time I saw him do something similar was on BBC One against Ray Floyd on the ninth green at the Belfry in the 1985 Ryder Cup.

After the morning pairs against Hampshire we were winning 3-1. In the afternoon singles we fell apart, with Way the only Sussex player to win his game. The rest of us lost and Hampshire won easily. I stood in the bar afterwards supping a beer and talking about the game with the Sussex senior captain, Mike vans Agnew. Mike pointed out Way through the bar window. After two rounds of golf, each taking four hours and comprising an eight mile walk, the *only* Sussex player to win both his matches that day was on the practice ground hitting balls for another hour.

Mike and I concluded that it was all about making choices: I chose to have a beer, Way chose to be the best golfer he could possibly be. The lesson I learnt that day wasn't that you had to practise to improve; I already knew that. What Paul Way taught me all those years ago was that no matter how good you are, you can always choose to work to be that little bit better.

A year after we were Sussex teammates, Way was winning his first professional golf tournament and my stab at making a living playing golf was finished. By August 1982 I'd chosen to go back to school and was deciding which A levels to study.

The case for all of us to improve our teaching

> People assume that the marginal gains idea is all about technology … It was more of a mindset and a philosophy that everybody in every little area of the team tries to improve what they are actually doing.
>
> Dave Brailsford

What follows is, fundamentally, really simple but it has its complexities too: it is only right for all of us to improve our teaching so that our students learn what we teach. No matter how good we might be at teaching, we always face the perennial challenge of being better – a challenge derived from Charles Handy's observation that, 'The paradox of success, that what got you where you are, won't keep you where you are, is a hard lesson to learn.'[1]

I deliberately use the word 'great' rather than 'outstanding' throughout this book. In many ways it makes complete sense to use the Ofsted description of outstanding teaching when we talk about what outstanding teaching looks like. But I don't use that word, and nor do parents or students, when they talk about the best teachers; such teachers are described as great teachers.

It may be semantic hair-splitting, but a commentator on my blog seemed to get to the heart of the matter when he wrote, 'Teachers are both artisans and artists, and both sides need to be fostered, otherwise we will just become excellent, soulless technicians.'[2] I think one of the key things to improving teaching is putting the student at the centre; great teachers with soul do this. They know each student well and are interested in them as individuals; this means that they plan well, understand what motivates students and develop their teaching to meet their students' varying needs because they understand what grabs them.

Great teachers observe, reflect, learn and make subtle but powerful changes to meet the needs of their students – a good example is the way that a great teacher uses questions to understand barriers to learning and reshapes their teaching to help individuals make progress. So, let's use great teachers; not outstanding, excellent or soulless technicians, but great teachers who put the student at the centre of things.

'Every teacher needs to improve, not because they are not good enough, but because they can be even better.' This line from Dylan Wiliam, in his keynote speech at the SSAT Conference in December 2012, has been important in shaping my argument about why all of us

---

[1] Charles Handy, *The Empty Raincoat: Making Sense of the Future* (London: Arrow Books, 1995).

[2] See comment at: John Tomsett, This Much I Know About … Why All of Us Must Improve Our Teaching No Matter How Good Our School, *John Tomsett* (5 January 2013). Available at: http://johntomsett.com/2013/01/05/this-much-i-know-aboutwhy-all-of-us-must-improve-our-teaching-no-matter-how-good-our-school/comment-page-1/.

must improve our teaching. Wiliam goes on to add: 'It has become a well-known mantra amongst school leaders, even if it elicits a sigh from many classroom teachers when uttered by school leaders who do not understand its implicit challenges for colleagues.'[3]

Wiliam built upon his argument for continuous improvement of teaching in his speech to the Northwest Evaluation Association's summer conference in 2013, when he said:

> The only way that we can improve teacher quality is to create a culture of continuous improvement. That is given lip service in many districts, but nobody is really facing up to what it really means in practice. You see, I think that every teacher needs to get better. In many districts they target help at the teachers who 'need support', who need help, who are having difficulties.
>
> Every teacher fails on a daily basis. If you are not failing you are just not paying attention. Because we fail all the time.
>
> Many of you will walk out of this room absolutely convinced I said stuff I know I didn't say. As teachers we fail all the time. We teach these brilliant lessons. We take in the notebooks and look at what the kids have written and we wonder what planet they were on when we were teaching the stuff.
>
> Our daily experience as a teacher is a failure. Which makes it the best job in the world. Because you never get any good at it. At one time, André Previn was the best paid film-score composer in Hollywood and one day he just walked out of his office and quit. People said 'Why did you quit this amazing job?' And he said – 'Because I wasn't scared any more.' Every day he was going into his office knowing his job held no challenge for him.
>
> This is something you are never going to have to worry about. This job you're doing is so hard that one lifetime isn't enough to master it. So every single one of you needs to accept the

---

[3] Dylan Wiliam, How Do We Prepare Our Students for a World We Cannot Possibly Imagine?, speech delivered at the SSAT National Conference, Liverpool, 4–5 December 2012.

commitment to carry on improving our practice until we retire or die. That is the deal.[4]

Wiliam delivers the speech with a certain amount of humour but his message is serious. Like Wiliam, I take it as a given that every single teacher wants to become a better teacher; indeed, to become a country of truly great schools we will all need to become better teachers, every single one of us.

I am not claiming that we have to work harder in terms of volume of work, but to work harder at becoming better at what we do in the classroom. I am saying that every single one of us has to be at least a good teacher and the majority of us truly great teachers. And that applies to all of us: I feel quite strongly that all members of school leadership teams should be respected practitioners who are at least consistently good and working towards becoming great teachers.

For some of us who have been teaching a long time, improving our practice will be difficult. According to Rivkin, Hanushek and Kain all teachers 'slow their development, and most actually stop improving, after two or three years in the classroom.'[5] But CPD means that we have to reflect upon our practice regularly and systematically.

An Enote teacher-blogger has written, 'Professionalism to me means always being willing to re-evaluate your practices when things don't go well. It also means being willing to learn from others. Of all the excellent teachers that I've seen over the years, the best shared a common trait: they always thought they could do better, and they always thought their colleagues, even first year colleagues, could teach them something worthwhile.'[6] This encapsulates why continuing

---

[4] Dylan Wiliam, Every Teacher Can Improve, speech delivered at the Northwest Evaluation Association Conference, Portland, OR, 26 June 2013. Available at: http://www.youtube.com/watch?v=eqRcpA5rYTE.

[5] Steven G. Rivkin, Eric A. Hanushek and John F. Kain, Teachers, Schools, and Academic Achievement, Econometrica 73(2) (2005): 417–458.

[6] Enotes, What Does/Should Professionalism Mean to a Teacher? (13 December 2011). Available at http://www.enotes.com/eduphilo/discuss/what-does-should-professionalism-mean-teacher-115966.

professional development has to be central to the job of teacher; we must commit to continuing professional development in the true sense of that phrase.

The flipside of Rivkin et al.'s observation is that there are many long-serving teachers in our school system who deliver no-frills good lessons, lesson after lesson, day after day. What they do is ingrained in their professional practice so deeply that they would struggle to explain why they are so effective. A challenge for school leaders is to engage with these seasoned practitioners so that they can surface what it is that is special about their pedagogy; if we can do this, then those teachers can contribute to developing younger colleagues. Chapter 14, in which I interview our longest serving teacher, Dave Lamb, is an attempt to make explicit the pedagogical practice which he does not realise he has mastered.

In order to stay focused on professional development we need to stop worrying about things we cannot control and focus upon what we can do something about – our own practice. The only way to develop truly great schools is through each one of us taking responsibility for improving the quality of our teaching. We need to break the glass ceiling which surrounds great teaching so that we all aspire to it and see it as achievable. We need to foster a growth culture which is founded upon the belief that all of us can improve.

For teachers to believe in a growth culture for themselves is difficult; however, it is difficult because teaching is seemingly inextricably linked with our personality. To accept that there is a flaw in our class-room practice can feel like admitting there is something wrong with us as a person. David Hopkins describes the debilitating link between personality and practice as 'the elephant in the classroom'. He bases his thinking around this on the ideas of Richard Elmore of Harvard University:

> Confusing people and practice is deeply rooted in the culture of schools, and it is especially resilient because it resides in the beliefs and the language of school people. We speak of 'gifted' or 'natural' teachers, for example, without ever thinking about

the implications of that language for how people improve their practice. If practice is a gift that falls out of the sky onto people, then the likelihood that we will improve our practice at any scale is minimal. There are only so many sunbeams to go around, and there aren't enough for everyone.[7]

What we must do is be open to the observation of our practice in order to develop it, and to ensure we challenge the practice and not the individual teacher. We must recognise the difference between *practice* and *personality*. The challenge is to expand our repertoires and take on new skills. In other words, to support colleagues as they take risks to improve their own classroom practice. Thoughtful tweaks to our teaching can have significant positive impact on student learning, as exemplified by Alex Quigley who, inspired by Zoë Elder's Marginal Gains website,[8] explains how the aggregation of marginal gains concept has enabled our own students to make accelerated progress in their learning.[9]

The other barrier to colleagues opening themselves up to improving their practice is accountability; as professionals, accountability is something we have to accept. As long as we know what is expected then we can eradicate the fear inherent in any accountability system. I want to catch colleagues doing good things and praise them, not catch them out. There have to be formal judgements made about the quality of teaching; we need to accept that and begin to shape performance management processes into our broader CPD systems.

The best way to make coaching, mentoring and lesson observations developmental is to focus on the impact of specific elements of our

---

[7] David Hopkins, Every School a Great School, speech delivered at Limestone Coast Region Leader's Conference, South Australia, 18–19 October 2010. Available at: http://www.docstoc.com/docs/167430533/ every-school---Department-for-Education-and-Child-Development.

[8] See http://marginallearninggains.com/.

[9] See Alex Quigley, An Unexpected Olympic Legacy: How to Make Marginal Gains With Your Students, *The Guardian* (22 November 2012). Available at: http://www.guardian.co.uk/teacher-network/teacher-blog/2012/nov/22/ olympic-legacy-marginal-gains-students.

practice upon student learning rather than obsessing with any judgement grade. If we accept that we can all improve then a judgement grade becomes unnecessary and irrelevant; improving our practice becomes the main focus.

We can and must accept that there is no one formula for great teaching – a view endorsed by Michael Wilshaw when he said to the RSA, 'We need to celebrate diversity, ingenuity and imagination in the way that we teach. Surely this is common sense when every child is different; every class is different, and every year group is different. One size rarely fits all. Surely this adage must apply to teaching as it does to most things in life.'[10] As long as we are teaching well, and that good teaching is resulting in students learning and making good academic progress, we will be doing a good job.

Finally, I think becoming a better teacher requires the individual teacher to have three key dispositions. First he needs an aptitude to teach. Second he needs to be open to learning – if he does not genuinely think he has more to learn about his practice then he will not move beyond having an aptitude for teaching. Third he needs to have the will to be a great teacher – the determination to be the best he can be. If each one of us in the teaching profession has these three dispositions then we will create a nation of truly great schools; but we are not going to improve our teaching by wishing ourselves to be better. And it won't happen if we just keep on doing what we have always done, hoping that by sheer effort we will improve.

Sheer effort doesn't make you improve, as Alex Quigley so brilliantly described in another article where he grappled with his inadequacy as a footballer:

> If I was to total my hours of practice it would surely be in the thousands. In fact, it would near the 10,000 hours total which has been associated with becoming an expert by people in the know. Only I am not an expert. I am little better than I was when I was a spotty teenager. A long time ago I stopped improving at football. I had reached my 'ok plateau'.

---

[10] Michael Wilshaw, What Is a Good Teacher?

He concludes that we all need to work hard to improve our practice in a supportive culture:

> I may be a bit past my dream of playing for Everton, but with the right type of practice and support I can improve to eventually become an expert teacher. When Dylan Wiliam popularises research that proves that students with the best teachers learn twice as fast as average then our pursuit of excellence, with effective coaching and deliberate practice, could just make a transformative difference for our students.[11]

It's important that Alex ends with the students. I've always believed that if you look after the school's culture, the examination results will look after themselves. Barth brilliantly highlights the connection between a thriving school culture, teacher development and student outcomes:

> When we come to believe that our schools should be providing a culture that creates and sustains a community of student and adult learning – that this is the trellis of our profession – then we will organize our schools, classrooms, and learning experiences differently. Show me a school where instructional leaders constantly examine the school's culture and work to transform it into one hospitable to sustained human learning, and I'll show you students who do just fine on those standardized tests.[12]

For us all to become better teachers we need to work in a culture where that is possible. Indeed, as I outline in Chapter 10, the single most important factor to us all improving our practice is the school culture.

---

[11] Alex Quigley, Overcoming the OK Plateau: How to Become an Expert Teacher, *The Guardian* (11 April 2013). Available at: http://www.theguardian.com/teacher-network/teacher-blog/2013/apr/11/expert-teachers-ok-plateau-professional-development.

[12] Roland S. Barth, The Culture Builder, *Educational Leadership* 59(8) (2002): 6–11.

This much I know about why you can always be that little bit better

- Assume that every teacher wants to improve their teaching – it's a powerful attitude which gains cultural currency over time.

- Demonstrate your own commitment to improving your teaching and be open about your moments of failure in the classroom.

- Promote the notion that there is no one formula for great teaching.

- When it comes to colleagues trying to improve their teaching, celebrate risk-taking publicly.

- Stop awarding judgement grades for individual lesson observations.

Chapter 3

Why I teach

The road not taken

> If you would have your son to walk honourably through the
> world, you must not attempt to clear the stones from his path, but
> teach him to walk firmly over them – not insist upon leading him
> by the hand, but let him learn to go alone.
>
> Anne Brontë, *The Tenant of Wildfell Hall*

I always wanted to be a professional golfer. In 1979 I had a week off
school to caddy for my brother's mate, Trevor, at the British Open Golf
Championship at Lytham St Anne's, just outside Blackpool. Trevor
was playing in the qualifying rounds a week before the event began for
real. As soon as we had secured a room in a bed and breakfast we
headed for the championship course.

We stood on the first tee at Royal Lytham alone. The organisers had
hardly begun erecting the stands. None of the course was roped off. As
we looked towards the first green a couple of people walked up behind
us. It was Jack Nicklaus and his caddie, Jimmy Dickinson. We exchanged
greetings. Just to repeat, it was *Jack Nicklaus* who was then, and still is
now, the most successful golfer who has ever lived.

For some reason I had a pen with me and I got Nicklaus' autograph, as
well as a can of lemonade he'd picked up months before at the
Australian Open. We walked and talked with him, but he had arrived
too soon and the course was not yet prepared for championship play.
After five holes he declared to Dickinson, 'James, these greens are too
slow,' bid his farewells and left.

As Nicklaus departed, a young Severiano Ballesteros arrived. He was
being tutored by Roberto De Vincenzo; we walked with them and
listened as they plotted Seve's way around the course. Ten days later,

via the car park on the sixteenth hole, Seve would be crowned champion golfer.

It was, as you might imagine, a life-changing afternoon for a golf-mad 14-year-old boy.

A year later I took my O levels and did pretty well. In the autumn of 1980 I embarked upon A levels in biology, chemistry and mathematics, but my imagination was shaping golf shots, not solving equations. I did very little work, there was an incident involving fireworks and in the December I was asked to leave school.

My mother imploded, my dad said very little. Mother had always had high aspirations for me; she had left school when she was 13, too ill to complete her education. In me she saw the chance to realise her intellectual potential by proxy. A postman, my father didn't want me to end up in a blue-collar job like him, and he knew how difficult it was to make a living playing golf.

In the winter of 1980 I began two years of working hard to be a golfer. I was moderately successful. I won the Sussex junior championship two years running, captained the under-18 and under-23 Sussex teams and played for the full senior team. A number of my peers went on to play in the Ryder Cup with Ballesteros; I ended up cleaning cars to subsidise my golf. In the end I didn't practise hard enough for long enough. I made a lot of what I had, but it wasn't what was required to forge a career.

Not making it as a professional golfer was one of the most important formative experiences of my young life. I learnt that to be good at anything you needed to work hard and be utterly disciplined. Having worked as a greenkeeper, painter and decorator and car cleaner, I had experienced the unrewarding grind of monotonous manual labour. If I didn't know it at 16, then I knew by 18 the importance of a good education. I'd had a go at following my dream. I had no regrets.

On Saturday 28 August 1982 at around 10 p.m., Cliff, the barman at the local pub, offered me a job behind the bar; on the following Monday I went back to school. Ron Hunt, the terrifying deputy who bid me farewell nearly two years before, agreed to give me a second chance, and I began my A levels again as my year group was leaving, choosing economics, English and mathematics.

Unpredictably, my A level English teachers, Marion Greene and Dave Williams, nurtured in me a love of literature, and at the University of York the likes of Sid Bradley, Pippa Tristram and Geoff Wall helped me to discover literary worlds I had never imagined, but not one that involved a classroom.

I didn't enter the teaching profession to teach. When I was close to finishing my English degree I faced up to the inevitable fact that I had to get a job. I wanted to get paid for discussing literature and the only way I could do that was to become a teacher.

Growing my teaching

> I may not have gone where I intended to go, but I think I have ended up where I needed to be.
>
> Douglas Adams

Peter Abbs was our English PGCE tutor at the University of Sussex in 1987–1988. 'Any student can learn how to punctuate through creative writing'; that's a parody, to an extent, but it has more than a grain of truth in relation to the core philosophy of Peter's book, *English Within the Arts.*[1] Peter is a deep thinking, fiercely intelligent academic who helped inspire me to write poetry. He taught in a school for three years in the mid-1960s and took up his first academic position as a research fellow at the University of Wales in Aberystwyth circa 1968.

We loved the way Peter talked: once he wanted us to sit in a semi-circle to watch a video and he said, 'Come and sit in a crescent shape … you know, I just can't stop talking symbolically!' The thing is, I learnt very little from my PGCE about how to teach.

---

[1]   Peter Abbs, *English Within the Arts* (London: Hodder Arnold, 1982).

I began my career teaching literature at Eastbourne Sixth Form College, which used to be the boys' grammar where *Dad's Army's* Captain Mainwaring was educated. I had five A level groups in my first year of teaching. It was blissful and it didn't seem like work. I was earning a living chatting about Shakespeare.

Like I said, I didn't enter the profession to teach. I didn't really think about teaching. I didn't think very hard about how I taught. I learnt a simple teaching/learning process intuitively. My first ever lesson as a qualified teacher was based on Edward Thomas' poem 'As the Team's Head-Brass'. I chose that poem because I liked it. My love of literature rivalled my erstwhile love of golf. I was getting paid for doing something I enjoyed doing. I wasn't cleaning or delivering letters.

I explained the context of the poem. I read it aloud to the students. I explained a small number of crucial aspects. I asked them to work in threes to identify the three voices in the poem and to prepare a reading for the rest of the class. I then asked them to identify ten questions about the poem they wanted answering, pared down the suggestions from the class to a single set of ten questions and asked them to attempt to answer those questions for homework. Next lesson, I went on to support them in writing their first A level literary criticism essay.

So I learnt to teach for real by being thrown in front of twenty youngsters who needed me to teach them well so that they had a chance of getting good enough A level grades so they might go to university. I reckon that my sheer enthusiasm for the subject, along with my positivity and work ethic, was enough for me to be an effective teacher. The students certainly attained good grades in their A level examinations.

If I did think about the teaching at all, I had the ambition to help the students to become active readers of the texts we studied. I certainly didn't look at a mark scheme or assessment objectives; if the students could ask good questions about why a writer had made certain decisions about how he or she had structured a text, and they could answer those questions, the rest would look after itself.

What's great is that I have learnt more about my English subject specialism since I have been a teacher than at any other time in my life. I came across a huge range of literature at a surface level during my degree at York and was inspired by the English department (1984–1987), which, as well as Sid Bradley, Pippa Tristram and Geoff Wall, comprised Jacques Berthoud, Derek Pearsall, David Moody, Nicole Ward-Jouve, Hugh Haughton, Bob Jones, Michael Cordner, Tony Ward, R. C. Hood, Stephen Minta, Hermione Lee and Alan Charity – the golden generation, a kind of academic Premiership Select XI with a cracking subs bench to boot!

However, it wasn't until I began my career at Eastbourne Sixth Form College and taught five A level classes in my first year that I began to comprehend fully the fundamental relationship between form and content which underpins the analysis of literary texts. I think I learnt my own core texts at A level in some depth, but nowhere near as well as I now know *The Winter's Tale*, for instance, a text I have taught a number of times.

Over the past twenty-six years I have built up a store of teaching and learning strategies which have helped students to gain great examination outcomes. I have had times when I have worked hard on my practice and other times have been fallow, when nothing new has developed and I have relied on what I know to work. I have been confident enough to teach a range of subjects, leaving English to teach mathematics and even A level economics.

In the past three years, however, some of my certainties about the teaching process have begun to wobble. I thought I knew how to teach. I thought I knew how children learn. Now I'm not so sure. And I'm not so sure because I'm thinking much harder about the whole learning process through working with the likes of Professor Rob Coe and Tom Sherrington as well as my colleagues at Huntington School. Such incredible educational thinkers have challenged not just me, but the whole profession, to reflect upon what we are doing in the classroom and how, to use Dylan Wiliam's now famous phrase, 'every teacher needs to improve'.

Much closer to the end of my career than to the beginning, I feel like I'm learning how to teach all over again and, second time around, it's much more interesting!

This much I know about why I teach

- The motivations behind why I teach have changed over the years; I used to want to teach only sixth-formers – now I think early years is probably the most important age group.

- I began teaching inspired by my love of literature, but now I'm driven to teach by a sense of moral purpose.

- I teach because no one day is the same; I may have taught iambic metre every year for a quarter of a century but it's all new to the students in front of me.

- One of my favourite questions at interview is, 'Why did you choose teaching?' One of the most probing questions I ask is, 'What annoys you about education?' Both have proven effective over the years.

- The bottom line is that to be any good at teaching it has to matter to you, properly, right there in your chest.

Chapter 4
Why writing matters

In my element

> Writing a book is a horrible, exhausting struggle, like a long bout with some painful illness. One would never undertake such a thing if one were not driven on by some demon whom one can neither resist nor understand.
>
> George Orwell

I have always had the urge to write. The first article I had published appeared in the *Sussex Express* in 1972 when I was 8-years-old. I wrote about hunting for antique bottles. We used to spend days on end digging out an old Victorian refuse dump searching for stunningly beautiful bottles. I wrote a piece for the paper which ended with a line about appreciating the beauty of a cobalt blue poison bottle for its own sake rather than worrying about how much money it might be worth.

By the age of 10, however, my obsession with golf meant my teens were spent aiming for a career on the European Golf Tour. The legacy of those years comprises some great memories, modest success and a right shoulder which hangs six inches lower than its counterpart. The love of the written word continued, however, and, when I left the fairways to return to studying, Seamus Heaney's poetry led me to study English at the University of York.

I dabbled in sports writing for a while. At university in the mid-1980s I studied amidst a number of budding journalists. David Conn, Andy Dunn and David Maddock have gone on to become nationally renowned sports writers. I once covered the West Ham v West Bromwich Albion game for Maddock when he was writing for the *Daily Star*; on that particular Saturday he was moonlighting for the *Independent* at Aston Villa v Derby County. Interviewing Lou Macari in the West Ham changing rooms, pretending to be a genuine hack was, as Sir Alex Ferguson would say, 'squeaky bum time'!

Maddock once asked me whether I thought he should change from journalism to teaching. I explained that teaching is a solitary business. Its magic moments are largely unacknowledged, occurring in distant corners of the school on wet February afternoons. It might be when a student understands how and why you use substitutions in algebra, or why Sonnet 18 is about Shakespeare's art rather than a love poem. Whatever it is, that moment of light-bulb-switching-on learning will be shared by only you and the student. Writing is not for the retiring type, and I told Dave that swapping his picture by-line in the *Mirror* for the relative anonymity of a corner of a classroom in a school amongst thousands of other schools in England wouldn't be for him.

In the early 1990s I was runner-up in a *Guardian* sports writing competition and met some of my journalist heroes at the modest awards event – Matthew Engels, Peter Preston and the late John Diamond. Predictably, the article was about golf and it prompted me, a few years later, to write to the editor of *Golf World* and challenge him to send me to Augusta to cover the US Masters golf championship; he didn't send me but went himself.

He did, however, commission me to write an article on junior golf in the UK which he published; I even got paid. The actual edition appeared on the magazine racks in Rita's newsagents in *Coronation Street* a few weeks later. The funniest thing about that article was my picture by-line's mistaken identity …

John Tomsett teaches at Hove Park School in East Sussex.

Between the commissioning and publishing of that *Golf World* article I had secured a teaching post in York. Instead of building upon that article I was consumed with my new role at Huntington School. Who knows where I would be now if I had managed to write the next piece for *Golf World*. Golf, writing, teaching – sometimes I'm still not completely sure I'm in the right job.

All of this – bar the odd poem I've had published – charts my writing career to date. As head teacher of Huntington School, I reckon I have one of the best jobs in the world, but when writing I feel like I'm in my element – a state Sir Ken Robinson describes as 'the point at which people feel most themselves and most inspired'.[1]

Teaching students how to write

> This is how you do it: you sit down at the keyboard and you put one word after another until it's done. It's that easy, and that hard.
>
> Neil Gaiman

I can remember having my first university essay marked. The lecturer had scrawled across the front page, caustically in red pen, 'You need to get a dictionary and use it', after I had written explaination [*sic*] in my opening sentence, but I can't remember being taught how to write essays at school or at university.

That said, I'm not sure how students, including myself, get to the age of 16 and appear as though they have never been taught how to plan an essay in their lives. I know for sure that teachers have taught students how to plan essays; it's clear, however, that the art of essay planning is difficult to learn. Too many students get to A level and continue to claim that they don't like to plan – 'I just write it'. The sense that writing is a craft which needs conscious development is one that by-passes too many students, despite the teachers' best efforts.

---

[1] Sir Ken Robinson and Lou Aronica, *The Element* (New York: Penguin, 2009).

The fact remains that explicitly teaching our students writing skills is an educational essential, especially essay-writing skills. Maybe too many students can't plan essays well because our teaching of the planning process has never been good enough. Teaching the art of essay planning is often a case of training students to:

- Underline the key words in the title.

- 'Thought-shower' their ideas.

- Group together similar ideas.

- Take each group of ideas as a paragraph.

- Put the paragraphs in order.

- Write the essay.

All underpinned by the ubiquitous PEE (point, evidence, explanation) paragraph structure. The odd mind map might be thrown in amongst the spider diagrams. Of course I generalise, but I bet I'm not far off the mark.

Writing good essays is increasingly important for students as our examination system demands a higher standard of literacy than has been required for a generation or two. All our students will need to have secure literacy skills, including the ability to write extended prose with coherence and clarity. If a good set of examination results is the best pastoral care for students from socioeconomically deprived backgrounds, then challenging all our students to become better readers and writers becomes a moral imperative.

In the past few years I have developed three strategies which, collectively, have helped my students to become better writers. The first is learning how to plan an essay, where I show students how to work backwards from a finished essay in order to understand how it was constructed and replicate the writer's original essay plan.

To begin, I present them with a beautifully crafted essay and ask them to uncover the author's essay plan. One of the essays I use is written by Magdalena Lomacka from the American International School,

Vienna.[2] The essay isn't word perfect; however, if you work away at the essay like an archaeologist works away at a delicate structure hidden in the ground, you'll unearth a priceless literary treasure. The essay title, 'Compare and Contrast Our Approach to Knowledge About the Past With Our Approach to Knowledge About the Future', invites open, rambling responses, but such a response would gain very few marks.

The students' essay is restricted to 1,200–1,600 words, and anyone who writes seriously realises that is very few words to shape a response to such an open essay title. But this constraint is a real advantage; it means the writer can waste not one word.

In a well-planned essay you will find the argument is summarised in about ten sentences. I ask the students to use a dreaded highlighter pen to identify the key sentences which, when strung together, will encapsulate the essay's argument. Again, I impose a limit of no more than a dozen sentences. Here is Magdalena's essay reduced from 1,600 words to fewer than 400 words:

In order to compare and contrast our approach to knowledge about the past and the future, I shall consider the methods and limitations of understanding them through the study of history, science and the arts.

If essential information regarding the same event varies depending on location and the time period in which it is studied, we must ask to what extent we really depend upon history to give us the truth.

Yet being acutely aware of one's history is so important, because from it we can extract wisdom valuable for making new decisions and predictions. [However] the limitations of forecasting include not only those already associated with attaining the knowledge of the past, but also the practical

2 Magdalena Lomacka, Compare and Contrast Our Approach to Knowledge About the Past With Our Approach to Knowledge About the Future. Available at: http://freegyan.org/downloads/TOK/50%20Excellent%20TOK%20 essays/ETOKE/html/essays.html.

issues that can arise in the future and that currently simply cannot be accounted for.

However, more precise forecasting seems to be possible by means of science, as scientific method allows us to make predictions that must be true if specified conditions are justified. In order to say that I know [something scientific], not only do I have to rely completely on the authority that has made the conclusion, but also assume that all its underlying assumptions are correct. Our approach to the knowledge of the future also relies on the predictions made by scientists, but these, just as the theories discussing the past, tend to alter due to new insights and are hard to rely on due to complexity.

Having discussed the methods and limitations of history and science, it is valid to discuss a more imaginative approach to our knowledge of the past and the future. [Human achievements] would never have happened were it not for abstract ideas of creative minds; in that sense, our creative approach to knowledge about the future creates it.

Ultimately, just as in history we use reason to assess evidence and try to limit emotional and cultural bias, so does scientific method aim to obtain objective knowledge of the past and the future. A final distinction could be made by the means of emotion, as our approach to the future can possibly be that of hope and determination to shape it.

It's a beautifully constructed argument; these 355 words are the essay's thread and are taken almost verbatim from the original essay. All Magdalena has done to complete her essay is provide specific, relevant examples to evidence her points, using a very light touch; she hasn't got enough words to allow herself to get bogged down.

Once the students have understood how essays are planned, they can move on to explicitly identifying other features of the text. In order to signpost the argument's thread, I teach students my second strategy: to begin each paragraph with a sentence which looks back to the previous paragraph's point and forward to the next point in the new paragraph.

The label I have used for this skill idea might just be original. When you move from one sentence to the next in an essay to achieve a sense of continuity, it helps if you begin the first sentence of the next paragraph with a 'Janus-faced sentence'. Now, in ancient Roman religion and myth, Janus is the god of beginnings and transitions and he had two faces which looked in opposite directions. Ever wondered why the first month of the new year is called January?

So, here's a student's example of the end of one paragraph and the beginning of the next which is enhanced by the Janus-faced sentence highlighted in italics. The essay compares Simon Armitage's poem 'Give' – about people living on the streets begging for money – with Carol Ann Duffy's poem 'Medusa', a sinister monologue from the snake-haired gorgon.

> The character in the poem 'Give' feels angry as well as bitter that a house owner has a house but he is without one: 'Of all the public places, dear'. Armitage emphasises the character's bitterness with the dramatic pause with the use of the comma to add sarcastic tone to the word 'dear'.
>
> *Whilst Armitage uses a sarcastic tone Duffy uses a more threatening voice*, and direct tone towards the man: 'Are you terrified?' The way she says 'you' she's making a point that she is just angry at him and there's no one else to get him out of it.

The Janus-faced sentence becomes a valuable shorthand for talking to students about shaping their essays. Magdalena's essay contains a number of such sentences which help build the skeleton of her argument:

> Having discussed the methods and limitations of history and science, it is valid to discuss a more imaginative approach to our knowledge of the past and the future.

Furthermore, at word/phrase level there are a number of lexical choices which help the reader to follow the argument: *in order to, if, yet, however, also, having discussed, ultimately.* This close level of analysis focuses students even more intently upon the art of arguing a case.

Exemplify each point and you have the plan. Nailing the argument thread in 355 words means that Magdalena has 1,244 words left to write about the well-chosen examples which evidence her key points. At this point the students are set the task of writing the essay plan, linking the key points in the argument thread to the examples. What they end up with, having dug carefully beneath the finished artefact, is the structure which holds it together and the place where the writer began.

I think Magdalena treats her examples with a beautifully light touch: 'Picasso's painting of Guernica surely is not an accurate account of how many people died in the massacre or of what they looked like.' What she assumes here is that the reader is on the same intellectual plane as her; she doesn't waste precious words explaining Picasso's *Guernica*, she just assumes anyone reading her essay will be familiar with the painting.

How can students produce truly excellent work if they don't understand the process by which such works are produced? Reading exemplar texts is one thing; digging away to unveil the original essay plan takes the students' understanding of how exemplar texts are constructed to a significantly higher level. Magdalena's clarity of argument is rooted in a thorough plan; the plan means that actually writing the essay is the easy bit!

Only when they have an understanding of the planning process of the best essayists can our students begin to produce work which reflects their own very best writing skills. Now, after my moment of originality, my students' first task when writing their own essays is to write their ten sentence argument-thread. Once they have the plan and the examples, the students then need to write the essay.

Writing with brevity and clarity requires practice. My third strategy represents one of the best ways I have found to sharpen students' writing skills – that is, to compose a group essay. Plan the essay with the class and allocate a paragraph per student, depending upon the number of students in the class. Set a deadline for email submission of the single paragraphs well before the next lesson so that you can paste together the single paragraphs to form the complete essay. This allows you to discuss the essay in an almost anonymous manner.

In the next lesson, I ask the students to work in pairs and we read through a randomly chosen paragraph projected on the whiteboard. I count the number of words and I set them the three-minute task of reducing the length of the paragraph by two-thirds whilst retaining its key information. I then annotate the paragraph on the whiteboard using a marker pen, with them contributing suggestions for redrafting as we work from sentence to sentence. Quite often during this first attempt I lead the thinking process for redrafting the paragraph.

I repeat the task on a new paragraph, but I take the redraft from a pair of students and type up the contributors' reduced paragraph verbatim. I make it competitive, with the winner being the pair that can use the lowest number of words whilst keeping the paragraph's main point.

I repeat the task for the third time with the students writing individually, analysing one student's effort on the board together. By this time there is no sense of embarrassment about having their work looked at collectively because they have already begun to improve their writing. The homework is to handwrite the original full essay, reducing its length by two-thirds whilst maintaining its central argument. I ask them to handwrite the essay because they will have to handwrite their essays in the examination.

Those three activities – unveiling the original essay plan, constructing Janus-faced sentences and practising writing with brevity and clarity – have had a hugely positive impact on my students' examination outcomes. The three-part process is especially good at helping students who have always struggled with extended writing to gain a decent mark on questions requiring lengthier responses.

This much I know about why writing matters

- Language is power; it's that simple and that important for our students.

- Being literate opens up the world for our students, so we have to privilege the development of literacy skills in all our classrooms.

- When I teach mathematics, students find more difficulty in understanding what a mathematical problem requires of them rather than the numeracy demands of the problem.

- Students have to be taught how to exert deliberate control over language; it is not an easy thing to do but it is doable.

- Time invested in developing students' mastery in writing will be rewarded when it comes to them being externally assessed.

Chapter 5

The team to lead teacher learning

The chance to fly

> The thing with kids is, if they want to grab for the gold ring, you
> have to let them do it, and not say anything.
>
> J. D. Salinger

If I wasn't playing golf in 1980, I was listening to punk rock. For me
there was nothing quite like being in the mosh pit as The Clash began
their set. The first live track I heard them play was 'Clash City Rockers'.
Those opening chords growled out across the Brighton Top Rank and
the surge of energy was raw, elemental and purifying.

In those days as a 15-year-old, I'd go down into Brighton paying a
child's fare on the bus and then get into the Top Rank as an adult. That
journey was literally and metaphorically a rite of passage; the first time
in the mosh pit and I was changed forever, a child no longer.

A couple of years ago the BBC repeated *Westway to the World*, the Don
Letts documentary on The Clash, awash with live footage.[1] As soon as
the credits rolled the phone rang. It was my sister: 'If I'd known where
you were going back then I'd have got mother to stop you!'

I recalled my sister's words when I texted my 16-year-old son who was
at his inaugural Leeds Festival – his post-GCSEs reward. Our 'conversation' went thus:

Me: How's the music?

Joe: Insane right in the mosh pit.

Me: Have fun!

---

[1] *The Clash: Westway to the World*, dir. Don Letts (Sony, 2000).

It took a lot for me to key that last response. I identified completely with Joe's apparent love of the dangerous edge of moshing, but I was driven to encourage him in his first experience of the mosh pit by something I think I heard Sir Ken Robinson say somewhere about the myriad of pressures upon us not to do what we want to do, to be restrained.

Take the age-old parental farewell to our children, 'take care': even in this most sensible and understandable phrase we attempt to prevent our sons and daughters from exploring the fascinating, risk-rich world. I have always tried to implore Joe to 'have fun' rather than 'take care', though the latter still pops out sometimes when he's out in a car with his mates. It's hard, but we only ever have our children on loan; you have to let them do it and not say anything …

Westward Ho! is a small village on the north Devon coast. At its heart is Royal North Devon Golf Club, the oldest club in England and one of the finest seaside golf courses in the world. It co-hosts the West of England Amateur Strokeplay Championship. In April 1982 I made my way west to play in this prestigious championship.

Mother bought me the National Coach tickets. I set off from Uckfield coach station early, destination Victoria. In London I changed and caught the Bristol coach. At Bristol I changed and headed to Taunton. From Taunton I caught the Bideford bus and from Bideford I walked the mile or so to Westward Ho! I stayed at what's now known as the Surfbay Holiday Park in my very own chalet.

I lugged my clubs and clothing bag along with me, played golf (badly), failed to qualify for the final two rounds, hung around and caddied for Robert Lee (who now fronts golf coverage on Sky TV), and made my way back to Sussex following the same route I had travelled three days before.

I made one five pence call home from a telephone box to confirm my safe arrival and that was it. I could have been anywhere on the planet. No mobile phones, no Skype, no FaceTime. Nothing but my 17-year-old self and what little nous I had. Though, by the time I had arrived home, my little nugget of nous had grown.

Were my parents negligent, letting me go gigging at the Top Rank and allowing me to travel to Westward Ho! alone, or did they give me the chance to fly?

A school leadership team for improving the quality of teaching

To a certain extent, a school leader's effectiveness in creating a culture of sustained change will be determined by the leaders he or she leaves behind.

Michael Fullan

I have been hugely fortunate to have been recruited by John Morris, Peter Bratton, Chris Bridge, Norma Taylor and Jonathan Leach, all of whom took a gamble when appointing me. I was young to be appointed at every stage of my career, and I learnt from those five people to take risks when developing young leaders. Importantly, I give young aspirant colleagues with leadership potential an opportunity to lead, but I know how far I can allow them to fall. For years I was the youngest on the Senior Leadership Team (SLT), even when I first became a head teacher.

If you are going to develop young leaders of teaching, you have to be comfortable about the genuine distribution of leadership. Alma Harris is good on this when she says, 'It was the strongest leaders most comfortable in their own skins who were eventually most able to let go of power, thus allowing for the decisions of others. They were more likely to distribute than merely to delegate and still less likely to micro-manage others' every action so as to deliver someone else's agenda.'[2]

Our premises manager, Jeff Poole, once challenged me at a SLT meeting when he openly questioned whether I genuinely distributed leadership, or whether I thought I did but in reality still micro-managed

---

2   Andy Hargreaves and Alma Harris, *Performance Beyond Expectations* (Nottingham: National College for School Leadership, 2011).

people. It was a learning moment for me, and what I realised was that distributing leadership means distributing responsibility and account-ability; anything else is just delegating tasks. Now I give Jeff everything to do.

So, returning to our theme, can we really structure schools so that improving the impact of teaching on students' learning is at its very heart? At the London Festival of Education in 2012, John Hattie said, 'We are the first to deny our expertise as teachers and it is killing us as a profession; where is the Royal College of Teachers? Why aren't your best teachers in charge of developing your schools?'[3] Hattie's comments now drive my thinking about school leadership.

At the time, I said on my blog that I was interested in creating up to a dozen internal Advanced Skills Teacher (AST) posts at our school; post-holders would be responsible for developing pedagogic prac-tice across the school and would be meaningfully involved in shaping future strategic developments. Over time that idea has changed, as with most good ideas, but its intent underpins our school leadership structure.

I believe that you need to change your school structures until improving the quality of teaching is the explicit outcome of every initiative. I think our leadership structure at Huntington School has the improvement of the quality of teaching at its very centre. There are six posts – head teacher, curriculum deputy, director of research, assistant head teacher in charge of performance development and the developmental posi-tions for school-based Initial Teacher Training (ITT) and growth mindset – which form a spine whose coherent focus is upon improving the quality of teaching. We have also recruited five highly trained expert teacher-coaches who have responsibility for providing more intense support for individual teachers to improve their practice.

---

[3] John Hattie, What Makes Great Teaching (A Global Perspective)? [video], London Festival of Education, 17 November 2012. Available at: http://visible-learning.org/2013/02/john-hattie-at-the-london-festival-of-education/.

Our leadership structure is the fruit of eleven years of intuitive trial and error; I have never worked with the same leadership team from one year to the next. When reshaping a team, however, the key is to tweak it so that it never has to be totally dismantled. Once the leadership team's core purpose is established and understood by all, the next task is to align the school's other structures with the focus upon improving the quality of teaching.

It's worth noting that school leadership has to be underpinned by effective management: there is nothing more irritating for a full-time teacher who teaches twenty-three lessons a week than an over-led, under-managed school. Any good head teacher knows that nailing the management detail makes for an effectively run school and gains respect from all levels of the organisation.

This much I know about the team to lead teacher learning

- Make sure your school leadership team is focused upon the core business of school – improving teaching and learning.

- Ensure that your leadership team are good teachers themselves.

- Look to build balance in your team and quietly succession plan.

- The leadership team has to remove all the factors which hinder colleagues from doing their job to the best of their ability.

- Management matters – be sure to pay attention to the day to day.

Chapter 6

Why we *all* have to teach

Authentic hard graft

Children go where they find sincerity and authenticity.
Eric Cantona

Tom Gibbins was a friend of my dad. He was a jack-of-all-trades. He had a working-class gumption that meant he was never out of work. During the difficult late 1970s and early 1980s he had a number of jobs – obediently following Norman Tebbit's diktat that he should literally get on his bike and look for work. Tom was a decent bloke and a Piltdown Artisan golfer like my dad.

Piltdown was made famous over 100 years ago by the fake skull, dubbed 'Piltdown Man', which its finder, Charles Dawson, claimed was the evolutionary 'missing link' between apes and humans. My dad was born in Lamb Cottage, just behind the Piltdown Man pub where our young golfing crowd used to drink.

On a Friday evening we would finish our beers at 11 p.m. and go down to the tiny bakery in nearby Newick where Tom worked. Tom had learnt to bake and we would eat chocolate eclairs whilst spending an hour bewitched by his dexterity with the dough; the creamy elastic substance was utterly obedient in his fingers and seemed alive. He threw me the dough once and it died the moment I caught it. Tom was a real expert.

What I remember Tom for most, however – beyond his baking, his slicked-back black hair, his roll-ups and his sense of humour – was a quiet word of warning. I must have been boasting about my golf, for he took me aside and said quietly in my ear, 'Don't be a big-head. People think they're tossers.' What he said was born out of love for me and I have carried it with me ever since. That said, on the odd occasion, I've still been a bit of a tosser.

Years later, Professor David Hargreaves issued a similar warning to a number of head teachers, one of whom was me, when he asked us, 'Is your rhetoric beyond your practice?' And Jim Collins, author of *Good to Great*,[1] rates wilful humility as the most important quality in a leader. Do what you say you are going to do; authenticity is so important.

Why head teachers should teach

It is not fair to ask of others what you are not willing to do yourself.

Eleanor Roosevelt

I feel utterly convinced that you have to teach, no matter how demanding the role of head teacher has become. And I don't mean cherry-picking the small Year 13 class; I mean teach the tough classes, team-teach, teach more than your allocated number of lessons as and when required, and teach out of your subject if necessary. Whilst I am gut-wrenchingly worried about the school's headline figures on results days, I always sneak a look at my own students' results first!

The thing is, my contention that head teachers should be good teachers is backed up by research. There are numerous studies which support my argument that head teachers should be centrally involved in developing teaching and learning as well as teaching themselves. Take, for instance, the analysis by Christopher Day and colleagues into the impact of school leadership on pupil outcomes. Second in the report's ten findings is the claim that 'successful school leaders improve teaching and learning and thus pupil outcomes indirectly and most powerfully through their influence on staff motivation, commitment, teaching practices and through developing teachers' capacities for leadership'.[2]

---

[1]   Jim Collins, *Good to Great* (London: Random House Business, 2001).

[2]   Christopher Day, Pam Sammons, David Hopkins, Alma Harris, Ken Leithwood, Qing Gu, Eleanor Brown, Elpida Ahtaridou and Alison Kington, *The Impact of School Leadership on Pupil Outcomes: Final Report*. Ref: DCSF-RR108 (Nottingham: University of Nottingham, 2009).

Then there's the work by Michael Fullan, who concludes in his workshop series, 'Leadership: Maximizing Impact', that one of the 'three keys to maximising the impact of the head teacher is to model learning and shape the conditions for all to learn'. Fullan claims that the head teacher does work to 'ensure that intense instructional focus and continuous learning are the core work of the school and does this by being a talent scout and social engineer, building a culture for learning, tapping others to co-lead, and, well, basically being a learning leader for all'.[3] My vision of headship is rooted in an extensive evidence base.

A little cited but brilliant book, *Student-Centred Leadership* by Viviane Robinson, focuses on one single issue: the golden thread from school leadership to student outcomes.[4] The book is stunningly good: I feel strongly that we haven't got the time, energy and resources to do things in school which don't have a positive impact on student outcomes. That doesn't mean schools have to become examination factories – far from it – but our leadership activities as head teachers in creating a culture for students and staff to thrive have to lead to improved student outcomes.

Robinson's conclusion, having surveyed the research on how leaders make the most meaningful difference in schools, was the proverbial music to my ears. The main message from the research on how school leaders make an educational difference to the students in their school is summed up by Robinson thus: 'The more leaders focus on their relationships, their work, and their learning on the core business of teaching and learning, the greater will be their influence on student outcomes.'[5]

I maintain that head teachers who are really doing their job effectively know this instinctively; what is so great about Robinson's book is the empirical evidence she uses to support this claim. Having reviewed a

---

[3] Michael Fullan, Leadership: Maximizing Impact (spring 2014). Available at: http://www.michaelfullan.ca/wp-content/uploads/2014/04/14_Spring_Maximizing-Impact-Handout.pdf.

[4] Viviane Robinson, *Student-Centred Leadership* (San Francisco, CA: Jossey-Bass, 2011).

[5] Robinson, *Student-Centred Leadership*.

huge body of research into this issue – why head teachers should teach – she identifies five leadership dimensions:

1   Establishing goals and expectations.

2   Resourcing strategically.

3   Ensuring teacher quality.

4   Leading teacher learning and development.

5   Ensuring an orderly and safe environment.

This is supported by three leadership capabilities:

1   Applying relevant knowledge.

2   Solving complex problems.

3   Building relational trust.

What is remarkable about her meta-analysis of the 199 research studies is the comparison of the effect sizes which indicate the average impact of each dimension on student outcomes. Leading teacher learning and development had an effect size of 0.84, twice the size of any of the other four dimensions.[6] An effect size of 0.84 is very significant in the world of the educational researcher; indeed, it is striking stuff, especially when you consider that an effect size of 0.4 is significant, even in the eminent educational researcher John Hattie's eyes![7]

What Robinson says resonates strongly with the thrust of my argument: it's as though she has unearthed the research to prove what I have come to know through twelve years of headship. There are many

---

[6]   "'Effect size' is simply a way of quantifying the size of the difference between two groups. It is particularly valuable for quantifying the effectiveness of a particular intervention, relative to some comparison. It allows us to move beyond the simplistic, "Does it work or not?" to the far more sophisticated, "How well does it work in a range of contexts?"' Robert Coe, It's the Effect Size Stupid!, paper presented at the annual conference of the British Educational Research Association, University of Exeter, 12–14 September 2002.

[7]   John Hattie, Visible Learning for Teachers: Maximizing Impact on Learning (London: Routledge, 2011).

points in Robinson's argument to support mine: for instance, she cites Matsumura et al.'s observation that the credibility of teaching head teachers is enhanced because 'teachers know their leaders have first-hand experience of what they are endorsing'.[8]

The main conclusion Robinson draws as to why the effect of head teacher as learner is so great on general student outcomes is that direct involvement in professional learning 'enables leaders to learn in detail about the challenges the learners face and the conditions teachers require to succeed'.[9] According to Robinson, this enables the head teacher to ensure that any obstacles to creating those conditions for learning can be overcome.

It all makes such sense. It's what I intuitively know to be true and it's all backed up by thoroughly sound research findings.

This much I know about why we all have to teach

- Teaching is *the thing* for all teachers, isn't it?

- A teaching head teacher has more authenticity in the eyes of her colleagues than a non-teaching head teacher.

- It is pretty difficult to lead teachers' learning if you don't teach yourself.

- What you learn when you teach as a head teacher enables you to help others improve their teaching.

- When head teachers teach we really are all in it together.

---

[8] Lindsay C. Matsumura, Mary Sartoris, Donna DiPrima Bickel and Helen E. Garnier, Leadership for Literacy Coaching: The Principal's Role in Launching a New Coaching Program, *Educational Administration Quarterly* 45(5) (2009): 655–693, cited in Robinson, *Student-Centred Leadership*.

[9] Robinson, *Student-Centred Leadership*.

Chapter 7

Teaching the tough classes

Treading the line

> Aye, you're neither one thing nor yet quite t'other. Pity, but
> there 'tis.
>
> Eloise Jarvis McGraw

Just before I was born, my parents moved from Parklands, the tough
estate at the far end of the village, to the last of six council houses on
School Hill, just a short walk from Maresfield Bonners Church of
England Primary School. Whether it is my home address or my place
of work, school has been a constant in my life.

The Bonners' population was socioeconomically diverse. It was there
I first trod that difficult line between being one of the lads and working
hard academically; it is a line I have traversed all my life. I played in the
football team, stayed on decent – if somewhat wary – terms with the
playground toughs and tried really hard in class.

On Saturday afternoons my elder brother, David, would take me up to
the recreation ground to play football with the boys from the estate.
Nicky was a great fighter and the kingpin. His brother Jon, in my year,
was menacingly quiet. Boxer, Reidy and Gilbert were the others who
formed the Parklands inner circle. Juggsy was a bit older and the
hardest of the lot.

Those weekend afternoons on Maresfield rec in the early 1970s were
where I learnt how to survive amongst hard-nuts. I never got into
fights, probably because I wasn't worth fighting. If I was threatened I
refused to react; my passivity robbed the potential pugilists of any
entertainment. I hung in there, playing footie, watching what went on,
noting how Nicky and his cadre dictated life.

The 1974 Maresfield Bonners Uckfield District under-10s
five-a-side winners. Back row (L–R): Gilbert, Ben the head
teacher's son, Jon, me; front row (L–R): Reidy, Nicky, Boxer

When we got to secondary school, I gravitated towards the smokers.
The trouble was I didn't smoke. All my family were smokers. Years later
I recall fleeing upstairs to watch *The Great Escape* on Christmas Day
afternoon when everyone else in the front room had lit up – being
sporty and detesting the smell, I've never even had a drag. Yet treading
the line meant me standing behind the groundsman's shed at break-
time looking on as my mates passed round the Rothmans King Size.

I was once caned with the rest of my smoker mates when we were
rounded up by the deputy head and his break duty team in a well-orches-
trated pincer movement. Remembering my 1970s secondary school
experience is like scanning a montage of scenes from the film *Kes*.

The contradictions of being a rebellious goody-goody extended to my
cultural life. I played golf for Sussex but loved punk rock. The first time
I got dragged into the mosh pit, when I saw The Damned at the
Brighton Top Rank in 1979, I was intoxicated. The next year I won the
Sussex Junior Golf Championship. As Browning wrote, 'Our interest's

on the dangerous edge of things. The honest thief, the tender murderer, the superstitious atheist' … the punk rock county golfer.

So, when I am faced with a group of cheeky lads, years of treading the line means I'm never fazed. I know just how their minds work, about their love of banter and the primacy of sport and music in their lives. Looking out over such classes is, in some ways, like staring into a mirror.

Teaching cheeky lads (how to write)

Our job is to teach the students we have, not the ones we would like to have.

Dr Kevin Maxwell

Another one of Viviane Robinson's comments grabbed my attention when she claimed that the most powerful way that leaders can promote collective responsibility is by providing professional learning opportunities that help teachers to succeed with the students they find most difficult, a finding supported by the research of Goddard, Hoy and Woolfolk.[1] My own experience would entirely support this claim.

In 2011 we withdrew fourteen C/D borderline disengaged Year 10 boys from their English classes and I taught them GCSE English language and literature. It was a win-win – they stopped disrupting others and they made real progress. To improve the boys' performance, I soon realised that forging positive rapport was crucial. I invested lots of time in developing a relationship with each boy. Getting to know about them personally, so that I had something to discuss with them during those idle moments when they were queuing at the door waiting for the change of lesson, or when I met them round school, was truly important. Knowing their culture contributed towards forming a strong relationship. The fact that I knew who John Cena was and how to do a chokeslam was awesomely good in their eyes.

---

[1]   Roger D. Goddard, Wayne K. Hoy and Anita Woolfolk, Collective Teacher Efficacy: Its Meaning, Measure, and Effect on Student Achievement, *American Education Research Journal* 37(2) (2000): 479–507.

I know it's unbelievably obvious but knowing my sport helped too. Of course I support Manchester United – I was born in Sussex. When we lost the league to City at the end of the 2012 season, I walked into the library for our lesson, Monday period 1, and the boys were standing in front of the newspaper rack pretending to read the centre pages of all the papers; every light-blue sports back page faced me in welcome.

No matter what the subject, I got them talking. They all had a story to tell. They loved to debate a subject. As a one-off, I sat them round a dining-style table, gave them a paper plate and asked them to write down one person they'd like to invite to have a curry. And then we had a group discussion about who would be on a shortlist of six; it worked beautifully. And if they could talk about their work but couldn't write about it, I used a Dictaphone whilst they were telling me about it; the transcripts were magical.

Lastly, in terms of building a classroom culture, I have based my whole career upon a line from Virgil, 'Success nourishes them: they can because they think they can' – a better version of Henry Ford's famous dictum. So every time there was a minor victory, we celebrated the effort they had made and the resulting outcome. I never, ever, ever, ever, ever diverged publicly from believing that every single one of them would get a minimum of a grade C. Not once. And I kept things competitive; I'm not averse to awarding hard cash in class.

One of the things I did which changed the dynamic of the class was teach the boys explicitly how to write creatively and then how to write criticism. The process was highly structured and I modelled writing for them; these boys needed to be trained in how to write, but first they needed something more inspiring than the AQA short stories anthology.

Helen Dunmore's 'My Polish Teacher's Tie' is a decent enough tale, but even when I provided pre-lesson piping hot Polish dumplings I couldn't grab their attention for more than a few minutes, so we went back to a sultry night in Kinshasa on 30 October 1974 and based a piece of creative writing on some great stimulus material. I chose Norman Mailer's account of the Muhammad Ali vs. George Foreman

Heavyweight Championship bout called *The Fight*[2] and Leon Gast's film of the same event, *When We Were Kings*.[3]

I gave them a task which forced them to use their imaginations:

> Write a detailed description of the fight from the point of view of one of the boxers. To help you, choose which boxer's point of view you are going to write from, then watch the fight again and think about what that boxer must have gone through. Think about it through our five senses. What does he hear? What does he smell? etc. You will be able to use Norman Mailer's writing to help you write your version of the fight.

I encouraged them to write raw first drafts. Jack Nicklaus advises young golfers to hit the ball as far as they can when learning the game, and when they get older they can keep the length of their golf shots but learn how to control them; it's much harder to be controlled and then strive for length later. The same applies to the students' writing – they should hit the ball as far as they can, metaphorically, when they write their first drafts.

I word-processed their drafts for them, verbatim. Two lessons spent with them ham-fistedly typing would have killed the process; I promise you this is worth the time investment.

I then taught them directly how writers choose words for impact. I don't think there are many better examples of the impact of redrafting than the first sentence of George Orwell's *Nineteen Eighty-Four*:

> FIRST DRAFT: It was a cold, blowy day in early April, and a million radios were striking thirteen.

> FINAL DRAFT: It was a bright, cold day in April, and the clocks were striking thirteen.[4]

---

2   Norman Mailer, *The Fight* (London: Penguin, 2000).

3   *When We Were Kings*, dir. Leon Gast (Universal Pictures UK, 2009).

4   George Orwell, *Nineteen Eighty-Four: The Facsimile of the Extant Manuscript*, ed. Peter Davison (London: Secker & Warburg, 1984).

Orwell removes the disyllabic 'blowy' and 'early' so that, except for 'April', the final version begins with monosyllabic bluntness; he could have chosen March instead, but remember, April is the cruellest month. 'A million clocks' is a vague exaggeration; he then considers 'innumerable clocks' which is struck out because it is horribly awkward and he finally chooses the monosyllabic, 'the clocks'. The eventual simplicity of the opening twelve words of the first sentence ensures there is no distraction from the sentence's unsettling climax of the clocks 'striking thirteen'. With this beautifully crafted periodic sentence, Orwell communicates to the reader that something is wrong with the world of *Nineteen Eighty-Four*.

What do these boys need to persist in when developing their writing skills? Duckworth's grit[5] or Csikszentmihalyi's flow[6] or Dweck's growth mindset[7] or resilience or whatever? In the end, I reckon students need grit and sometimes they'll achieve flow. I think that if you teach them well they will approach writing grittily; then they will find they can write, when before they thought they couldn't, and you'll get flow, manifested in the occasional remark, 'Is that the end of the lesson already?'

I think there is one thing that all students need for them to feel engaged with their learning. Fundamentally students need to feel loved and I really don't care what anyone might think of that, to be honest, because if I know anything about teaching, I know that it's true. It's that simple and that complicated to convince colleagues of such a truth.

Tom, the leader of that group, felt loved and produced a stunning piece of writing:

---

[5] Angela L. Duckworth, Michael D. Matthews, Christopher Peterson and Dennis R. Kelly, Grit: Perseverance and Passion for Long-Term Goals, *Journal of Personality and Social Psychology* 92(6) (2007): 1087–1101. Available at: http://www.sas.upenn.edu/~duckwort/images/Grit%20JPSP.pdf.

[6] Mihaly Csikszentmihalyi, *Flow: The Psychology of Happiness* (New York: Harper Perennial Modern Classics, 2008).

[7] Carol Dweck, *Mindset: The New Psychology of Success* (New York: Robinson, 2012).

George Foreman

I came out second, jogging, feeling confident. The crowd was chanting, 'Ali, Ali, Ali!' Nothing could break my confidence. I entered the ring ducking and weaving, catching the crowd's attention; they were having none of it. The crowd was shouting, 'Ali Bumboyay!' He had no chance.

I could taste victory mixed in with sweat and Vaseline trickling down my face. The bell rung and my back were still turned. I turned, Ali was there dancing right in front of my eyes. He swung a few fast punches and missed. 30 seconds into the first round, he caught me with a right hand lead. I knew Ali's trademark was his speed but I couldn't believe it, he made me feel like a swatted fly. No one else had ever landed one on me!

Ali's pupils were bulging and the Vaseline smeared across his eyebrows had turned into slimy goo as the heat rose into his head. Fire built in my belly. I crazed; doing all I could, landing punch after punch in his face and in the ribs. I could feel the vibrations tingling from my fist, straight up my arm, and his nose merging into my knuckles felt a dream. His groans bellowed down my ear as I landed rib shot after rib shot. He teased me down my ear, 'Your punches aren't hard enough!'

Bell rung and we was now at round five. I was tired. I had a feeling Ali was off down this round, I could feel the victory. His face was swollen and his eyes were closing. He was all over the place like a drunken man, swaying out the ring as if he was leaning out of the window looking onto a roof, then I snapped, my head went. I was like a bomb on the last five seconds ready to explode. After each punch I threw I could feel the power building. I had no accuracy.

My stamina was decreasing after every breath I took; I felt dizzy and then … BOOM! It was like I got hit by a boulder, right in the jaw! I could feel my feet going from underneath me. BANG! POW! THUD! I could feel, see and hear the punches travelling into my brain as each punch cut into my face like a hot knife through butter. My adrenaline was high; I could not feel the pain until I saw the blood trickling from my nose. Then he landed the last punch. That was it. My feet had gone. I tried to hold up on Ali's shorts but I went, just like a tree that had been chain-sawed. I hit the ground and could barely hear the count. My mind and ears could work out 6, 7, 8, I tried getting up. I had no chance!

The crowd went wild! I was a defeated man. Ali bounced around the ring, getting pats on the back and congratulations from every angle as the ring got raided. My trainer got me up and took me into the corner. The last thing I saw was a wet sponge coming into my face.

So what did teaching that group for fifteen months achieve? First and foremost, nearly 70% of the boys attained two C grades in their English GCSEs. Their grades contributed to the best English language GCSE A*–C pass rate ever at the school of 84%; the GCSE literature pass rate was 91%.

As important as the hard student outcomes was the cultural effect it had on the school as a whole. Colleagues would chat with me about how best to teach some of our most challenging students. Some of the things I did, because I knew they were the best things to do with these students in the circumstances, made colleagues feel supported; for instance, I didn't bother setting homework whose completion was essential. Doling out punishment for incomplete homework detracted from the precious time I had with them in class – the time when I could influence what they did and how they thought. They completed homework badly, if at all, and then I wasted time writing in their planners at the beginning of the next lesson, when a sparky start was crucial if they were going to learn anything. So I set extension homework, having made sure all the essentials were covered in lesson time. I let my idiosyncratic homework policy be known publicly and colleagues felt relieved; some confessed they'd done the same thing but lived in fear of being found out.

My experience resonates with the research Robinson cites in her book: my direct involvement in teaching the most challenging students had 'enabled me to learn in detail about the challenges the learning presents and the conditions teachers require to succeed'.[8] Moreover, my colleagues saw me as a source of instructional advice.

The other happy outcome of refocusing my professional attention back into the classroom was the pleasure it brought me personally; I had a lot of fun teaching those boys.

This much I know about teaching the tough classes

- Boys fart. A lot. Just don't react. Or if you do, shout 'Doorknob!' dead quick. That stops it. (See page 68 for a full explanation.)

- Laugh with them and let them laugh at you.

- Trust them. Choose your moment and use the phrase, 'I'm going to trust you to do this,' looking directly into their eyes. It works.

- On some things you have to compromise. I know it encourages learnt helplessness, but just buy a stack of biros and don't get precious if you lose a load.

- Give them structure and establish routines. For instance, make finding their work as easy as possible. Even if you are the guardian of their work 99% of the time and you rarely let it out of your sight, that's OK because at least they'll have their notes to revise from in May of Year 11.

- Don't drive on with something just because there is a specification to get through it if it's clear you are draining them.

- Don't give them individual copies if you are analysing texts – use a single copy on the board so you know who's looking at what.

---

8   Robinson, *Student-Centred Leadership*.

- Feed them a lot. Stupidly it took me ages to work this one out. I knew my own son wasn't worth talking to if he was remotely hungry; when I made the connection I threw all the cake I could find at the problem.

- Construct as many learning tasks as you can that get them moving around the room. They have to get rid of that energy somehow.

- A reprimand now and again does no harm whatsoever. They're boys – as long as you're fair, they'll be fine.

- Let them know you know what they think they know. And always be the adult.

- Apparently, if you're an adolescent male and one of your mates farts, if you shout 'Doorknob!' before he shouts 'Safety!' you can hit him as hard as you like until he has touched the handle of a door, hence 'Doorknob!'

Chapter 8

Explanations

How did I end up here?

Life is what happens while you are busy making other plans.

John Lennon

I like the film *Sliding Doors*, where the main character, Helen, a London PR executive, is fired from her job and rushes out to catch a train and two scenarios take place. In one, she gets on the train and comes home to find her boyfriend in bed with another woman. In the second, she misses the train and arrives after the woman has left. In the first scenario, Helen dumps her boyfriend, finds a new man and gradually improves her life. In the second, she becomes suspicious of Gerry's fidelity and grows miserable.

Sliding Doors explores the road not travelled. I don't think you can be properly human if you haven't wondered what might have happened to you if you had, at a certain moment in your life, made a different decision. Where could you have ended up? What if? As the widely quoted Socrates' saying goes, 'True wisdom comes to each of us when we realise how little we understand about life, ourselves, and the world around us.'

When I arrived at York in October 1984 I could not have anticipated such a thing only four years before. In September 1980 I had embarked upon biology, chemistry and mathematics A levels. I was, essentially, a scientist. But I hadn't got the golf thing out of my system and to have persisted with an education at that moment would have been fruitless. I left school in December 1980, making a brandy-fuelled farewell speech at the sixth-form Christmas disco.

When I returned to school two years later, I had forgotten the basics of the sciences but I could do mathematics. I didn't need the O level to take A level economics and was left scratching around for a third A level. English literature was the only reasonable option open to me.

What I realise now, as a head teacher, is that David Williams and Marion Greene – my two great English teachers – were partnered for a reason; they complemented each other perfectly. Dave was an incredibly thorough teacher. When we studied *Mill on the Floss* we pored over every word – and there are quite a few of them. Once Dave enquired as to how long there was left of his own lesson. When one of us replied, 'Thirty-five minutes', he put his head on his desk in despair; even he was bored.

The thing is, Dave's thoroughness was a genuine strength. I knew all the texts we studied cover to cover. Marion was the opposite. She taught us like we were university undergraduates. If you didn't work outside the lesson to supplement what grains of genius you managed to glean from a Greene lesson then you were lost. Luckily, she inspired me and taught me Heaney's poetry – I still have a book of Irish verse with her name inscribed on the inside cover. And it was Marion who had been to the University of York to study English.

At York I met Pete. Pete was from Denton in Manchester. He was first-generation university like me. He was into sport like me. He was from a working-class family like me. And he had a friend called Louise from Ashton-under-Lyne sixth form who came to visit from Durham where she was studying. We all went out. Pete left Louise with me whilst he went to work at the all-night garage.

Louise and I have been married for twenty-six years and have two boys, Joe and Ollie. Now, Pete was a canny bloke who never did more than he needed to; he had researched all the sociology degrees across the country before completing his UCAS form. He put York top of his list because the assessment regime was the easiest by far – eight 3,000 word essays and no examinations. In the end our mate, Len, wrote three of those essays for Pete.

So, am I here today because of Marion Greene's testimonial, or because whoever set up the sociology degree course at York was an examination-phobic, or because my break from academia meant I ditched the sciences? Or was it because Lloyd West, my Year 9 tutor, said I ought to choose a modern language in my options and my CSE grade 1 in German met the entry requirement for the English and related literature degree course at the University of York? Or am I here because I wasn't Seve Ballesteros?

I think you can overanalyse; some things are just inexplicable.

My top three classroom explanations

If you can't explain it simply, you don't understand it well enough.

Albert Einstein

I think explaining concepts with clarity is one of the most important skills required of a teacher. Just for fun I have included here how I teach three quite different concepts which students find challenging to learn.

Explaining film genre theory in media studies

Language has so many limitations and most of the time we explain things through metaphor and simile; we use comparisons expressed in other words to explain something rather than explain that something itself using its own terminology.

For a film to be classified in a certain genre it has to contain a well-defined, familiar set of key features; the same as with a tin of baked beans. And when we think of baked beans we automatically think of Heinz Baked Beanz. So, the key features of a tin of baked beans which form the definitive concept of baked beans are: the beans, the tomato sauce and the pastel blue tin wrapper with the strapline 'Heinz Baked Beanz'.

Mainstream film is all about industry profits. Imagine releasing the first ever tin of Heinz Baked Beans on an unsuspecting public. You've kept that product secret for months and suddenly, *boom!* It captures the whole of the 'orange teas' market in hours. Commercial joy. (Orange teas was what we called tea in the 1970s when you got home from school and your mum either couldn't afford, or couldn't be bothered, to serve up anything other than a tin of beans, spaghetti or ravioli on toast – the orange refers to the colour of the food.)

Commercial competition drives innovation in film genre. Imagine you're the head of R&D at Crosse & Blackwell. Your tinned ravioli sales plummet overnight. What to do, what to do? You change your production line so that it produces your own baked beans following the exact same formula as Heinz, except for the pastel blue tin wrapper and that irritatingly good phonetic strapline. And you recover a decent share of the orange teas market.

To keep a genre commercially viable and interesting to your audience you tweak the well-defined, familiar set of key features, adding something new to the next film whilst clearly maintaining the genre classification. The bosses at Heinz are gutted. With Crosse & Blackwell's beans on the market profits have dropped. What to do, what to do? Answer: develop a new product which is still undeniably Heinz Baked Beanz but with a twist on the original – Heinz Baked Beanz with Pork Sausages! Still Heinz, still baked beans, but with a difference which will attract new buyers. And, hey presto, profits rise again and you steal back most of the orange teas market that you lost to Crosse & Blackwell.

Film genre production is cyclical. Bosses at Crosse & Blackwell respond with their own Baked Beans with Pork Sausages. Heinz retaliates with Curried Baked Beans. And so it goes on until every variation on the original Heinz Baked Beanz has been developed.

Keeping within the limits of the genre is important. There are moments when the well-defined, familiar set of key features are tweaked so much that the new product is almost unrecognisable as Heinz Baked Beanz – Heinz Baked Beanz Pizza, for instance – but throughout the production cycle the definitive, pure concept of baked beans – the beans, the tomato sauce and the pastel blue tin wrapper with the phonetic strapline – is recognisable.

Film genre cycles tend to end where they began. As the product is exhausted, Heinz decide to promote the original product once again as there will be customers who have forgotten what plain old Heinz Baked Beanz tasted like; they re-establish the product which began the whole product cycle all those years ago. If the original bolsters sales again the cycle will repeat itself.

Once students understand the metaphorical explanation of something they find the real thing easy to understand. The heist movie genre is a gift to teach. It is a sub-genre of the gangster movie and is nicely demonstrated by the following eight films:

- *The Asphalt Jungle* (Huston, 1950) – the blueprint for all heist movies.

- *Rififi* (Dassin, 1954) – variation: the twenty-eight minute dialogue-free safe-cracking scene.

- *The Killing* (Kubrick, 1956) – variation: parallel narratives.

- *The Taking of Pelham One Two Three* (Sargent, 1974) – variation: hold-up on a tube train.

- *City on Fire* (Lam, 1987) – variation: set in Japan with a police insider.

- *Reservoir Dogs* (Tarantino, 1991) – variation: the heist movie without a heist, in real time.

- *Ocean's Eleven* (Soderbergh, 2001) – variation: hi-tech trickery and a remake.

- *Heist* (Mamet, 2001) – as the title suggests, a definitive heist movie of the old school.

If you want to study one film then make it *Reservoir Dogs*, as it steals from all that came before it: *The Killing* (parallel narratives), *The Taking of Pelham One Two Three* (the colour nicknames), *High Noon* (real time) and *City on Fire* (insider police officer and several iconic moments – for example, Keitel's eye-level double gunning down of the police car is taken directly from Lam's film). And it does the most audacious thing: it contains no heist and yet it is a heist movie. Tarantino shows that you can remove the main element of the genre's recipe and still keep the movie rooted unmistakably within the genre.

If you want testimony to the effectiveness of this method of explaining film genre theory, it surely lies in the fact that in one mock examination essay on film genre one of my students cited the baked bean theory of film genre with some authority.

Explaining generic narrative structure

Despite the threat of being lampooned by Michael Gove when he was secretary of state for education – remember what he did to the Mr Men historian[1] – I use the film *Toy Story* to illustrate the generic narrative structure of most stories which is simply: order–disturbance–complication–resolution–new order.[2]

Nearly every student you teach has seen the first *Toy Story* film. It is perfect for teaching narrative structure because it follows the order–disturbance–complication–resolution–new order linear structure perfectly. Illustrate the linear structure graphically and relentlessly use the terminology of narrative and soon your students will be analysing the narrative structure of the most challenging novels with sophistication and confidence.

Explaining the law of diminishing returns in the short run

This is much simpler than the title suggests. In economics there are four factors of production: land, labour, capital and entrepreneurship. In the short run at least one of the factors is fixed. This means that productivity declines as the non-fixed factors are increased. Lost? Well, this is how I explain the law of diminishing returns in the short run.

---

1 Jessica Shepherd, Michael Gove Attacks Use of Mr Men in iGCSE History Lessons, *The Guardian* (9 May 2013). Available at: http://www.theguardian.com/politics/2013/may/09/michael-gove-mr-men-history-lessons.

2 *Toy Story*, dir. John Lasseter (Disney, 1995).

Set up the classroom so that eight tables form a square with a space in the middle and an access point in the corner. Place four chairs inside the square, one on each side of the square. This is your building (i.e. land in economic terms) and the four seats are four hi-tech computer terminals (capital in economic terms). I have had the idea for a website design company called Websett (entrepreneurship in economic terms). In this case these three factors of production are fixed. I cannot expand the physical space of the company (land), I cannot afford any more computer terminals (capital) and Websett is at the very limits of my creative thinking (entrepreneurship).

The students comprise labour, the fourth factor of production, and I get them to stand outside the square of tables. The first employee enters the company's work space and sits down at a seat. He creates eight websites a week. When the second employee enters she creates ten websites a week because she talks with the first employee and they learn new skills from each other. The third employee creates twelve websites a week. When the fourth employee is recruited he creates sixteen websites a week. Altogether they create forty-six websites a day and the students each have a computer terminal at which to work. When the fifth employee enters the 'room' he has to stand around because there are only four terminals. He only creates nine websites a week. The sixth employee is even less productive as it begins to get a bit cramped in there. And so on.

What appears quite a dry, theoretical concept suddenly becomes very tangible as you flood the work space with student employees and they realise first-hand why, in the short run, a company will, at a certain point, suffer diminishing returns as a single factor of production is increased when all the others are fixed.

To these students, the graph overleaf will make total sense.

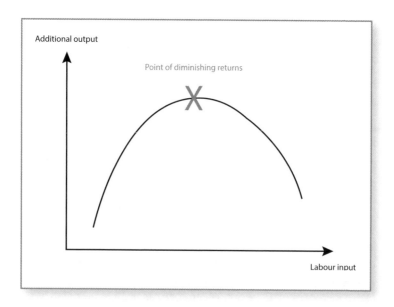

This much I know about explanations

- Less is more: pare down what you are explaining and make it as simple as possible without it becoming simplistic.

- Have more than one way to explain something – just because you can understand your way of explaining a concept doesn't mean that all your students will be like you.

- We mostly explain things in terms of something else; metaphors are useful (as the baked bean theory of genre illustrates) but try hard to use subject-specific vocabulary at all times.

- Ask students to explain your explanation back to you to ensure that they have understood.

- Return to explanations on a regular and relatively frequent basis so that the students move them from their short-term memory to their long-term memory.

Chapter 9

Lessons

Learning lessons

> In school, you're taught a lesson and then given a test. In life, you're given a test that teaches you a lesson.
>
> Tom Bodett

The early autumn of 1980 was hot. It was perfect weather for wasting time and that September there was, quite suddenly, lots of time to waste.

No one told us about private study. Without any preparation, it was left to us to decide what to do with all those lessons when we didn't have a lesson. Why would a group of 16-year-old lads like us, who had done moderately well in their O levels, have any idea what to do with what seemed like endless undirected hours? Honestly.

We spent a great deal of time in the bus station cafe, quite probably the grimmest place for a cup of tea imaginable. It was so awful that they were pleased to have any custom, even if it was a group of spotty teenagers sharing one cuppa and smoking. At other times we went back to my house at the bottom of the road from the school to play cards. There we got into cutting our own hair in front of the kitchen mirror. I popped into the common room one morning with a semi-skinhead, much to the disappointment of my soon to be ex-girlfriend.

One particularly mindless pastime was killing wasps with our bare hands. The warm autumn saw the wasps out in droves, dopey but still dangerous. We congregated around the waste bins. You had to stun the wasps with a clap and then kill them by squashing them between your fingers. Ann Pearce, the mathematics teacher, caught us culling the jaspers and thought we needed to see a psychiatrist, so odd she found our behaviour.

Wednesday afternoons were for outside guest speakers. We had a number of people come to cast their pearls before the sixth form that autumn, none of whom I can recall. What I do remember was the particular Wednesday afternoon that spelled the beginning of the end of my first attempt at A levels.

I'd already been chucked out of chemistry and had planned to find the teacher, apologise for my blatant disinterest in the lesson and see if he would let me back into class. Instead I found myself hanging around in the boys' toilets, just outside the main doors to the sixth-form common room where our latest guest speaker was orating, with my mate Brophy. Brophy had just been to France. France meant really loud bangers. Bangers meant trouble.

We plaited the fuses of four bangers together so that they essentially became *une grande pétard*. I lit it and we stood behind the cubicle doors. The explosion was loud. In the aftermath you could hear reactions from other teaching blocks across the way. I looked out the window and saw bullet-headed Tudor Jones leaving his classroom with some urgency.

Brophy locked the cubicle door and stood on the toilet pan so you couldn't see his feet. I left the toilet, stood outside and began idly perusing the noticeboards, innocence personified. Tudor pushed past me and after some Welsh bawling left with his hand round the scruff of Brophy's neck.

To be fair to Brophy he never grassed on me. He was excluded there and then. On top of the chemistry misdemeanour, the wasps and the general lack of industry, my role as the suspected accomplice in the infamous toilet bombing was enough for a stern letter home to mother.

About a week later I went to see Reg Winstone, our head of sixth form. He'd come into school despite writing off the school minibus the night before. As blood oozed from the deep wound on his forehead, he agreed that it was probably a good idea that I should leave. He gave me the line about only regretting in life what you don't do, which was enough to convince me that my A levels were all over. I did think at the time that he probably regretted crashing the minibus into the lamp post, considering the blood, his black eyes and how he had to retch into a bucket halfway through our conversation.

So that was it. I had slipped off the line I had trodden since I'd been at primary school. I was out on my own and winter was coming; the last one had been the infamous Winter of Discontent and what approached was no more promising.

At the time, quitting my A levels felt an 'audacious, purifying, elemental move', as Larkin so eloquently put it in his poem 'Poetry of Departures'.[1] But I was about to learn my lesson: Margaret Thatcher was in power, unemployment was rising rapidly and I had just added to the jobless figures.

Planning lessons

> Let our advance worrying become advance thinking and planning.
>
> Winston Churchill

I've only met Tait Coles once, but we got on well enough because I was the only person in his audience at Pedagoo London 2013 who had seen The Damned live; I saw them eight times in all, the first time in 1979 and the last time a couple of years ago, on their thirty-fifth anniversary tour.

Tait's book, *Never Mind the Inspectors*, propounds a revolutionary approach to teaching and I admire his belligerent tone.[2] It reminds me of a line by Jacob Bronowski: 'It is important that students bring a certain ragamuffin, barefoot irreverence to their studies; they are not here to worship what is known, but to question it.'[3]

---

[1]   Philip Larkin, 'Poetry of Departures', in *The Less Deceived* (Hull: Marvell Press, 1955).

[2]   Tait Coles, *Never Mind the Inspectors* (Carmarthen: Independent Thinking Press, 2014).

[3]   Jacob Bronowski, *The Ascent of Man* (London: BBC Books, 2011).

In the preface to his book Tait says, 'There isn't an aesthetically pleasing proforma that will enable you to plan a punk learning lesson in five minutes. How can teachers even consider that something planned in five minutes is going to be worthwhile? What can you actually plan in five minutes? Making toast? When and where to have a dump?'[4]

Of course Tait is correct. And he's correct not just for punk learning lessons, but for all lessons. Teaching is simultaneously simple and complex. To cater for the different learning needs of each student in a class of thirty individuals is a hugely complicated, time-consuming task and, I would argue, near impossible to achieve.

Like Tait says, planning a decent lesson takes more than five minutes. In a school which lives by the mantra, 'working harder makes me smarter', there is no short cut to planning teaching which maximises students' learning. Yet there is a small number of core teaching practices, like effective questioning, which are essential to all good lessons.

Unlike Tait, we do have a pro forma for planning all lessons – it is called a 'lesson map', which sounds like jargon, but is explained by the idea of getting from York to Leeds. I'd normally use the A64, but sometimes it's blocked by a road traffic accident so I have to go via Tadcaster and Boston Spa. But I'll get to my destination one way or another. The same applies to lessons – I know where I want to end up, but I'm not sure, when I start the lesson, which route I'm going to take. As Biesta says, 'Whether someone will be taught by what the teacher teaches lies beyond the control and power of the teacher.'[5]

I make sure I have several paths I can follow depending upon the way the students' learning takes shape during the lesson. We make our own teacher planners rather than buying commercial versions so that our lesson maps are used by all our teachers. The main space is for teachers to note a number of options for teaching that lesson, and therein lies the freedom and creativity desired by teachers. We all know that

[4] Coles, *Never Mind the Inspectors*.

[5] Gert J. J. Biesta, Receiving the Gift of Teaching from 'Learning From' to 'Being Taught By', *Studies in Philosophy and Education* 32(5) (2013): 449–461.

lessons are often derailed by the context of that group of students on that particular day in that particular lesson.

The key behind the lesson maps is knowing who is in front of you and planning for those students accordingly. That is why lesson plans written in a scheme of work are not enough on their own – class 9R3 last year was not populated with the same students as class 9R3 this year. And that is why we have class lists which identify key information about the students and that help us to plan lessons to meet the learning needs of as many of them as possible.

Schools are full of data about students, much of which is functionally useless. However, we have begun using reading ages in Year 7 and Year 10 as a key indicator of academic capacity; just that one piece of information on our set lists is really helpful for lesson planning.

Once you know who is in front of you, it is then possible to plan the accurate targeting of your questions. I had a telephone conversation with Dylan Wiliam in 1998, the week after *Inside the Black Box* was published.[6] He said, 'In England we spend preparation time marking, in Germany they practise the exposition and in Japan they think up good questions.' He still repeats this mantra, and he is dead right about the importance of good questioning.

I love Michael Fullan's thoughts on the power of the humble checklist,[7] which was the inspiration for the checklist at the top of our lesson map (see page 83), and which I think is a powerful element of the pro forma. Fullan cites the surgeon-writer Atul Gawande who says, 'Checklists are quick and simple tools aimed to buttress the skills of expert professionals.'[8] Quite. Our checklist hardwires in teachers' minds the thinking required to help support individual students' learning.

---

[6] Paul Black and Dylan Wiliam, *Inside the Black Box: Raising Standards Through Classroom Assessment* (London: GL Assessment, 1998).

[7] Michael Fullan, *Change Leader, Learning To Do What Matters Most* (San Francisco, CA: Jossey-Bass, 2011).

[8] Atul Gawande, *The Checklist Manifesto: How to Get Things Right* (London: Profile Books, 2010).

When planning it is good to avoid jargon: 'lesson objectives' or 'learning outcomes'? I don't think anyone really knows. I sometimes ask this question at interview, and one candidate admitted he did not know and was fed up with his PGCE tutor insisting that he writes both on his lesson plans. We just use the phrase, 'What do you want your students to learn in this lesson?'

Why did we adopt the term 'plenary' to describe the end of the lesson? Its etymological root hardly suggests its meaning in the context of lesson planning. I think this is another term which has made the lesson planning process sound unnecessarily complex. 'Activity to ensure that you and the students both know they have made progress' seems a better way of describing what we need to plan for at the end of the lesson.

There has to be a sense of freedom when planning. I do not want to see timings on lesson plans. Timings on lesson plans are the devil's work! I see too many car-crash lessons where the teacher knows some students have not understood a key point but she drives on because she feels compelled to stick to the timings on the lesson plan; it is so unnecessary.

And how can you plan next week's lessons before you know how this week's lessons have panned out? The idea that you can have a scheme of learning on the virtual learning environment which gives you lesson-by-lesson plans is nonsensical. Using last year's lesson plan when in front of you are this year's students isn't logical.

Here's one of my lesson maps for a Year 12 theory of knowledge lesson on ascribing artistic value to works of art, which I circulated to all my teaching colleagues to exemplify how a lesson map might be used. It is clear that the map is in some ways an aide memoire for me as the lesson progresses; it prompts me to do a lot of thinking before the lesson and to anticipate what might happen during the lesson before the lesson begins. The lack of structure in the map section frees me to use my professional judgement as the lesson progresses.

I emailed my lesson map to all staff and provided six key tips on using lesson maps to clarify how to use them and how to ensure the maps enhance lesson planning:

1   There is no need whatsoever to write down the names of all the special educational needs and disability (SEND) students in the class on each lesson map; you have that information on the class list. What you might write down is the name of a student who said nothing last lesson and you want to find out why, or the students who missed last lesson and need to catch up.

2   The checklists are there to support your thinking. That thinking will be done as you are planning activities in the light of who is in front of you. They're just a note to self.

3   The main planning box on the lesson map is a brief note to self about what you might do in that lesson. If you have prepared a sequence of PowerPoint slides to illustrate a point, then just write 'PPT' on your lesson map – you know what the thinking is in your head about how you deliver it, and much of that will depend upon who is in front of you.

4   Because you know who is in the room, you might note who you want to question and exactly how you might phrase the opening question(s). How the questioning then develops will rely upon your questioning skills.

5   If you have a lesson plan in a scheme of work which details the activities you might use in that lesson, don't write out those activities in the main planning box on the lesson map! Just put 'see attached'. The main planning box on the lesson map is where you will note the adaptations to that prewritten plan in order to cater for the learning needs of those students in front of you.

6   Lesson maps should require you to write no more than you used to write before we introduced lesson maps. What they should do is get you to think harder about who is in front of you and help you meet the learning needs of as many students as possible. For instance, if you're doing group work, how you plan the composition of the groups will be a crucial thing to note down on your lesson map.

In a response to my blog on lesson planning, someone replied: 'At last someone else who shares my lesson planning technique. List of places to go, how we get there depends on the class.' This summed up to me the whole point behind lesson maps. It's hard to plan more than a few days in advance because you never know exactly where you are going to get to in any particular lesson.

I have no qualms about insisting that teachers use the lesson maps on a lesson-by-lesson basis. Planning lessons is the fundamental activity of any professional teacher. But when it comes to planning lessons, we are in danger of strangulating creativity in the classroom.

Over the past twenty years we have made tremendous progress in teaching, and in many ways practice in our state schools has never been better. However, over-planned lessons are a curse. One candidate for a post at Huntington had a lesson plan a full nine pages long. He could not teach because he was too obsessed with what his plan said he should be doing every two minutes. And more experienced teachers are losing confidence because they think there is some secret formula for teaching great lessons for which they have not been trained.

This much I know about lessons

- When planning lessons, begin with knowing who is in front of you.

- Assessment should help you plan for your students: mark–plan–teach–repeat.

- Expect the highest levels of attainment from every single student.

- Keep flexible and ditch the timings.

- Plan for fewer activities, which will encourage deeper learning and result in better student outcomes.

Chapter 10

Creating the conditions for growth

My natural world

Great farmers know what the conditions for growth are and bad ones don't.

Sir Ken Robinson

The chapter in Steinbeck's *Cannery Row* where Mack and the boys cull thousands of frogs on the captain's farm made me laugh out loud when I first read it: 'never in frog history had such an execution taken place.'[1] It is a scene similar to the first time I went out shooting rabbits as a very green junior greenkeeper.

I grew up in the countryside. For me, as a country lad who had been potato picking on his hands and knees for sixty-five pence a day, the seasons are ingrained in my psyche. As February gives way to March and the golf season gets underway, the weather conditions are vital. If it is relatively mild and damp, the better the grass growth; the more grass, the more chance the greenkeepers have of producing good greens. A cold, dry spring, on the other hand, and the greens will be thin and bumpy. Good greens depend upon the conditions for growth being just right.

I spent my university summer holidays working at the golf club as a greenkeeper. Up at 5 a.m. and finished by 2 p.m., I loved it; sometimes, in these difficult educational times, an hour's carefree grass-cutting would do for me quite nicely. At sunrise I'd take the hose and sprinkler, set them watering a green and nestle down in a bunker for a nap. Occasionally I'd wake to find the green awash. Cracking colleagues, the

---

[1] John Steinbeck, *Cannery Row* (London: Heinemann Educational Books, 1979), ch. 15.

smell of freshly cut grass and an indelible suntan were the free perks of a great job.

My sense of the natural cycle was heightened by being a golfer. Any serious golfer is obsessed with the conditions of the greens and the highly manicured patch of grass surrounding the hole. If the greens are anything less than perfectly flat and true, putting becomes more difficult. Really good greens are a delight; bad greens will mar any game of golf.

One of the biggest threats to the all-important greens at Piltdown was a plague of rabbits which nibbled the grass and left the greens in a mess. The head greenkeeper Ken's solution involved an old Skoda, a plank of wood and two 12-bore shotguns.

Ken cut a hole in the car's roof, dispensed with the bonnet (the engine was in the back of the car), removed the glass from the two rear-door windows, fed a car-width plank through the glassless spaces and secured it above the back seats of the car. No longer a Skoda, it was transformed into a gun-turreted rabbit extermination machine. Ken drove, I sat next to him, whilst Nigel and John perched on the plank, guns cocked.

At sunset we set out. My job was to pick up the rabbits and sling them into the car's bonnetless front. The furry green-defilers fulfilled every cliché about how they react when trapped in headlights. The first night was a massacre. I remember it as being far more enjoyable than it really should have been, in the same way that, post frog cull, the captain in Steinbeck's book was doubtful whether he had 'ever had so much fun'. At the end of the evening I was taught how to paunch and skin a rabbit. Summers spent as the junior on the greenkeeping team were a fine supplement to my academic education.

Understanding the natural world, then, was an essential feature of my formative years. On reflection, it should be no surprise that I have a keen sense of the importance of getting the conditions for growth right if we are going to thrive.

The culture for growing great teachers and successful students

Reculturing is the name of the game. Much change is structural, and superficial. The change required is in the culture of what people value and how they work together to accomplish it.

Michael Fullan

The one thing that destroys the energy of a workplace culture is a climate of fear. Conversely, people's energies are maximised when they feel loved and safe. Love wins over fear every time. Ron Berger has never been so right when he says, 'Culture matters'.[2]

There is good research to support such a standpoint. In 1982 Purkey and Smith argued that 'an academically effective school is distinguished by its culture: a structure, process and climate of values and norms that channel staff and students in the direction of successful teaching and learning'.[3] Furthermore, in their appositely entitled paper, 'Good Seeds Grow in Strong Cultures', Saphier and King say, 'If we are serious about school improvement and attracting and retaining talented people to school careers, then our highest priority should be to maintain structures that nurture adult growth and sustain the school as an attractive workplace.'[4] Schools have to be about the growth of both students and staff; indeed, in Chapter 18 I explain at greater length how to tend your staff so that they grow professionally and personally.

One of the greatest thinkers about effective organisations was W. Edwards Deming. He is best known for his theory of management for improving both quality and productivity through the application of his

[2] Ron Berger, *An Ethic of Excellence: Building a Culture of Craftsmanship With Students* (Portsmouth, NH: Heinemann, 2003).

[3] Stewart C. Purkey and Marshall S. Smith, Too Soon to Cheer? Synthesis of Research on Effective Schools, *Educational Leadership* 40 (1982): 64–69.

[4] Jon Saphier and Matthew King, Good Seeds Grow in Strong Cultures, *Educational Leadership* 42(6) (1985): 67–74.

fourteen points for managing organisations and the elimination of what he dubs 'seven deadly diseases'.[5] Deming is renowned for his work with the Japanese after the Second World War and is credited with being the inspiration for what has become known as the 'Japanese miracle' of the 1950s and 1960s. The Deming Way certainly worked.

In a little known but brilliant book on leading schools, called *The School for Quality Learning*, Donna Crawford, Richard Bodine and Robert Hoglund outline how Deming's approach to management could be applied to education.[6] Deming's eighth point for the effective management of an organisation is, 'Drive out fear. No one can put in his best performance unless he feels secure.'[7]

In *The School for Quality Learning*, in the section on point 8, there is a line which I wish I had written because it encapsulates everything I've ever thought about the culture we require in schools: 'Until educators accept the fact that fear and quality work are incompatible, there can be no real improvements in the quality of the educational system.'[8] Amen to that! So this chapter is all about creating a school culture which is fear free, 'where intrinsic motivation is understood, is valued, and is the inspiration for learning'[9]

Sir Ken Robinson advocates an agricultural model of education where the teacher is like the farmer, providing all of the needed ingredients and leaving the crop to grow and thrive.[10] In the same way that great teachers grow great students, the SLT has to replicate that process for

---

[5] W. Edwards Deming, *Out of the Crisis* (Cambridge, MA: MIT Press, 2000 [1982]).

[6] Donna K. Crawford, Richard J. Bodine and Robert G. Hoglund, *The School for Quality Learning: Managing the School and Classroom the Deming Way* (Champaign, IL: Research Press, 1993).

[7] Deming, *Out of the Crisis*.

[8] Crawford et al., *The School for Quality Learning*.

[9] Crawford et al., *The School for Quality Learning*.

[10] Ken Robinson, Developing Imagination in Education [video], lecture delivered at Full Sail University, Orange County, FL, 25 March 2008. Available at: http://www.youtube.com/watch?v=Tt055yb1YNg.

growing great teachers: 'We have to change from the industrial model to an agricultural model, where each school can be flourishing tomorrow.'[11] Sir Ken Robinson's philosophy about getting the conditions for growth right in our schools rings true to me.

Quite often I find valuable leadership guidance in sport. In the summer of 2014, Saracens Rugby Football Club enjoyed some success, much of which its CEO, Edward Griffiths, puts down to what is termed, the 'cult of Saracens'. In an interview, Griffiths said: 'Too much of sport operates under the tyranny of the result … the core principle at Saracens is that we gather talented people together, treat them unbelievably well and in return they try unbelievably hard. That is it.'[12]

Whilst I am absolutely clear that student outcomes are the most important measure of the impact of teaching, in an educational world increasingly dominated by performance league tables every school could do with adopting the 'cult of Saracens'.

Wayne Jones led the English Department at Hove Park School in the 1990s. He returned from a conference one day with a gift for me. It was a quotation describing Roland S. Barth's 'idealised school culture'. It reflects the key themes of Barth's must-read book, *Improving Schools from Within*.[13] He gave it to me because he imagined it would be like the kind of school I might lead one day:

---

[11] Ken Robinson, Bring On the Learning Revolution!, *TED* (May 2010). Transcript available at: http://www.ted.com/talks/sir_ken_robinson_bring_ on_the_revolution/transcript?language=en.

[12] Mike Henson, Aviva Premiership Final: Inside the 'Cult of Saracens', *BBC* (23 May 2014). Available at: http://www.bbc.co.uk/sport/0/rugby-union/27536258. It is worth noting that before taking up his role with Saracens, Edward Griffiths was chief executive of the South African Rugby Union. He has been credited with ensuring that the 1995 World Cup-winning Springboks side learnt all the verses of the new national anthem, 'Nkosi Sikelel' iAfrika', and coming up with the slogan 'One team, one country'.

[13] Roland S. Barth, *Improving Schools from Within: Teachers, Parents, and Principals Can Make the Difference* (San Francisco, CA: Jossey-Bass, 1991).

A Personal Vision of an Idealised School Culture
– Roland S. Barth

I would welcome the chance to work in a school characterised by a high level of collegiality, a place teeming with frequent, helpful personal and professional interactions. I would become excited about life in a school where a climate of risk taking is deliberately fostered and where a safety net protects those who may risk and stumble. I would like to go each day to a school to be with other adults who genuinely wanted to be there, who really chose to be there because of the importance of their work to others and to themselves. I would not want to leave a school characterised by a profound respect for, and encouragement of, diversity, where important differences among children and adults were celebrated rather than seen as problems to remedy. For 190 days each year, I would like to attend an institution that accorded a special place to philosophers who constantly examine and question and frequently replace embedded practices by asking 'why' questions. And I could even reside for a while in a laundry dryer if accompanied by a great deal of humour that helps bond the community by assisting everyone through tough moments. I'd like to work in a school that constantly takes note of the stress and anxiety level on the one hand and standards on the other, all the while searching for the optimal relationship of low anxiety and high standards.

From the day I received Wayne's gift over two decades ago I have had it pinned on my office wall. It seems to me to encapsulate the kind of purposeful, thriving community where we would all like to work.

During term time I spend over ten hours a day at work, and as head teacher I choose to spend that time in a place where the sound of laughter is commonplace. Don't get me wrong, I'm no David Brent from *The Office*, but I do like to work in an environment where we get on with things with a great deal of humour.

Barth is a great school leader. He has written about developing school culture at length and no more insightfully than in his essay, 'The

Culture Builder', where he says, 'To change a school's culture requires mustering the courage and skill to not remain victimised by the toxic elements of the school's culture but rather to address them.'[14]

When leading a school I think there are pivotal moments when the head teacher can make a decision which has an inordinate effect upon school culture – way beyond anything one imagines at the time of making the decision.

When I left Huntington School I was unhappy. I knew that, in the words of Gandhi, 'What I thought, said and did were not in harmony.' I had been socialised by the culture of the place almost without realising it. When I did realise just how socialised I had been it took me by surprise.

Three weeks into my first headship at Lady Lumley's School, a Year 11 assembly, and James swaggers in late with a newly acquired skinhead haircut. In very public terms I order him to about-turn and wait outside my office. I was imposing the culture of my old institution where I was deputy head teacher on my new school where I was in charge.

Halfway through delivering an Alex Ferguson-style hairdryer rebuke, something I had seen done many times at Huntington, James said quite calmly, 'You're not talking to me like that,' and walked out of my office. I was left pleading pathetically with him, 'Please come back, I'm really sorry.' In that moment I learnt that each school has its own culture and that imposing a culture upon a school will never work. Certainly, the culture at Lady Lumley's needed to change, but cultural change takes concerted, conscious effort, not shouting rebukes.

When I returned to Huntington School as head teacher four years later I had learnt a great deal about leadership. I looked back and realised just how green I was when I began headship.

Before I began as head teacher at Huntington I made several preparatory visits. One was to spend time talking with students about the school. One of the things they hated was the Orange Card Campaign

---

14   Barth, The Culture Builder.

(OCC). Now, the OCC was an extreme response to a feeling amongst the teaching staff that students were being defiant.

If what the students said was true, the OCC was a bit like imposing martial law or detention without trial. It was like the Special Patrol Group of the early 1980s where you could be picked up on the street under the new 'sus' (suspected person) laws. Essentially, if students were in any way defiant, or perceived to be defiant, a teacher would write on their recently distributed Orange Card and that would result in the loss of breaks and lunchtimes for a fortnight. The OCC was imposed in May, just when the school year can become a bit frayed, and the students loathed it.

Nearly a year into my headship at Huntington and the clamour for a new OCC began; colleagues felt that students were answering back too much. I thought about what to do for a week and then, at the whole staff Friday briefing, I explained to my colleagues what we were going to do in response to our students' behaviour. My spiel went something like this:

> Several colleagues have asked me to implement another Orange Card Campaign. People feel that students are being difficult, answering back and being defiant.
>
> Well, I've spent the last week thinking about what we do, and I've decided that we are not having another Orange Card Campaign. And this is why … First, if the Orange Card Campaign was effective in changing students' behaviour we wouldn't need another one – it clearly doesn't work and it is a short-term solution to a more profound problem.
>
> And second, an Orange Card Campaign is not aligned with our core purpose and our values. It's on the person spec for teenagers to be difficult. Always has been. And if we meet their aggressive behaviour with aggression we will escalate things. No, we're not having an Orange Card Campaign because that does not fit with the direction I want to take this school.

Instead of an Orange Card Campaign we will have a Celebrating Student Achievement Fortnight. Members of the SLT will visit as many classrooms as we possibly can and ask you to point out to us students who are working hard and have achieved well recently, students who we can celebrate rather than chastise. That epitomises the culture I want to create at Huntington School and it is the opposite of an Orange Card Campaign.

At the end of the fortnight I surveyed teachers and over three-quarters of them wanted the Celebrating Student Achievement Fortnight to continue. It was a key moment in changing the culture of the school.

Too many schools, and Huntington was, to some extent, one of them, are schools where, in Barth's words, lurking beneath the culture there is a 'chilling message': 'It goes something like this: Learn or we will hurt you. We educators have taken learning, a wonderful, spontaneous capacity of all human beings, and coupled it with punitive measures. We have developed an arsenal of sanctions and punishments that we inextricably link with learning experiences.'[15] It takes the head teacher and the SLT to lead a school's cultural change, and often that means taking a stand against the prevailing orthodoxy.

What happened to me and our school chimes precisely with Barth's observation that 'Achieving [a] better way [of doing things] takes recognition of and moral outrage at ineffective practices, confidence that there is a better way, and the courage and invention to find it and put it in place.'[16] During the eight years since my public rejection of the Orange Card Campaign, the SLT has both exhibited and insisted upon behaviours which have reflected our three core values – respect, honesty and kindness.

We changed from a school where the sense of threat was tangible – one science technician told me on her exit interview that before we had changed the culture of the school she wouldn't cross the school at breaks or lunchtime with an equipment trolley for fear of what the

[15] Barth, The Culture Builder.
[16] Barth, The Culture Builder.

students on the corridors might do to her – to a school with a learning culture where everyone feels safe and the vast majority are keen to learn. One of our December 2013 Ofsted inspectors remarked at the end of the inspection that he hadn't seen one student off-task in the whole two days.

When it comes to leading change Barth has a rival – I am also a huge fan of Michael Fullan. I make no apology for being a Fullan disciple. What I have found with Fullan is his uncanny knack of articulating in theory, with a great range of examples, what I have learnt intuitively as a school leader in practice. My leadership of change at two schools has taught me many things, most of which Fullan articulates in his book, *Leading in a Culture of Change*.[17] Here are his six guidelines for thinking about the change process which, to me, are plain common sense:

1   The goal is not to innovate the most.

2   It is not enough to have the best ideas.

3   Appreciate the implementation dip.

4   Redefine resistance.

5   Reculturing is the name of the game.

6   Never a checklist, always complexity.

So much of what Fullan says here I discovered the hard way, through first-hand experience; perhaps one has to live through professional strife before one can accept that Fullan-style wisdom is true.

Where, for example, Fullan says quite clearly that when implementing change, 'Reculturing is the name of the game', that is utterly congruent with what I have learnt about leading change through the Orange Card Campaign. Furthermore, he claims elsewhere that, 'The single factor common to successful change is that relationships improve. If relationships improve, schools get better. If relationships remain the same or

---

[17]   Michael Fullan, *Leading in a Culture of Change* (San Francisco, CA: Jossey-Bass, 2001).

get worse, ground is lost.'[18] This is genius dressed up in the plain garb of common sense. Teaching depends upon forging great relationships with students – when one thinks about it, it's obvious that successful change will depend upon improving relationships.

Finally, when he says that 'the first sixth months or so of implementation might be bumpy' he's wrong – the implementation dip can last a lot longer than that for a new head teacher. I call it HIDE (head teacher implementation dip excuse) or 'explanation' if you're feeling a little more charitable.

An aphorism which I often cite comes from Seneca, who said, 'The first step towards making a person trustworthy is to trust them.' I discovered that line in Clive Stafford-Smith's 'This Much I Know' feature in the *Observer* magazine.[19] Stafford-Smith's lifetime spent working for death row convicts suggests he knows a great deal about how people work, and I reckon Seneca was equally perceptive about the human psyche.

In my experience, the great myth about teachers – that they are a bunch of lazy pinko-lefties and paid-up members of Michael Gove's 'Blob'[20] – is just that, a great big myth. It couldn't be further from the truth. The vast majority of teachers I have worked with have been diligent professionals dedicated to doing all they can for their students. So, if they are free for the last period of the day, let colleagues go home if

---

[18] Michael Fullan, The Change Leader, *Educational Leadership*. Special issue: *Beyond Instructional Leadership* 59(8) (2002): 16–21. Available at: http://www. ascd.org/publications/educational-leadership/may02/vol59/num08/ The-Change-Leader.aspx.

[19] Ursula Kenny, This Much I Know: Clive Stafford-Smith, *The Observer* (18 December 2005). Available at http://www.theguardian.com/ theobserver/2005/dec/18/magazine.features7.

[20] Richard Garner, What Is 'The Blob' and Why Is Michael Gove Comparing His Enemies to an Unbeatable Sci-Fi Mound of Goo Which Once Battled Steve McQueen?, *The Independent* (7 February 2014). Available at: http://www. independent.co.uk/news/education/education-news/what-is-the-blob-and-why-is-michael-gove-comparing-his-enemies-to-an-unbeatable-scifi-mound-of-goo-which-once-battled-steve-mcqueen-9115600.html.

they want to. Trust them to get their work done when they choose; it's about being treated – and trusted – like professionals.

This much I know about creating the conditions for growth

- A head teacher can only be as good as the relationships she forges with her colleagues.

- Endlessly ask yourself, 'If I was having to implement this policy as a full-time classroom teacher, how would I feel about it?' It will help with your decision-making.

- The smallest kindnesses help everyone get through a full teaching day.

- It's not your idea, it's the best idea – and that might be hiding anywhere in your school.

- Always, always, always say thank you.

Chapter 11

Developing a growth mindset environment

A growth mindset by any other name

It took a few hard knocks in life to make me realise the only thing my dad had ever wanted or worked for was to give me a chance at being better than him.

Tucker Elliot, The Rainy Season

Sons are boomerangs – they leave you in their teens and come back to you in their mid-twenties. I'm afraid I was exactly twenty when my dad died, the point on my boomerang parabola of life most distant from him. However, I learnt a great deal from my dad, Harry, in the short time I knew him.

Dad was a really good golfer, and like any good golfer he was great at chipping and putting – that's the bit when you get near the flagstick and have to get the ball inside the four-and-quarter inch hole! You can hit the ball 300 yards with a drive but it counts the same as tapping the ball into the hole from an inch away. A shot is a shot.

So, to be a good golfer you need to be an expert chipper and putter. And the gentle joke everyone told about my dad was this: when the Second World War broke out Harry was chipping and putting round the twelfth green, and when the war finished he was still chipping and putting round the twelfth green! I heard people at the golf club tell that tale about dad repeatedly and the fact was that he was bloody good at chipping and putting.

Dad lived right next to the twelfth green and as a youth he would spend hours every evening practising getting the ball into the hole in as few shots as possible. It helped that the twelfth green was the trickiest green on the course, with many humps and hollows, giving him the opportunity to invent a range of chip shots unsurpassed amongst all the other players.

What I learnt from my dad, then, was that if you were going to be any good at anything you had to practise and practise and practise. I committed to golf when I was 10 years old. I played every day in the summer holidays and practised seven hours a day until my hands bled. I gave up studying at 16 to try to make it in golf professionally and spent hundreds of solitary days hitting shot after shot into empty skies.

Four things enabled me to become a scratch-handicap golfer by the age of 16, a full county player by the age of 17 and Sussex Under 18 Champion two years running: I was given an old set of clubs for free when I was 6; my father was friends with John Amos, the teaching professional at the club and an expert coach, the man who knew my golf game intimately; my dad and my eldest brother were single-figure golfers long before I began learning the game and we played together frequently; and I had easy access to cheap facilities at the Piltdown Artisan Golf Club for working-class golfers, enabling me to practise every single moment I could. By the time I was in my mid-teens I had invested Gladwell's 10,000 hours and some.[1]

All this came back to me when I read the opening to Matthew Syed's *Bounce*.[2] He credits his success at table-tennis to having the basic facilities, a great coach, an elder brother to compete with and a modest club with twenty-four hour access. His story was illuminatingly familiar. And thinking back, as well as the four-part recipe for success, for me it was also about the culture: the twelfth green myth of my dad, a background steeped in working-class grind and a belief that if you put the effort in you'll be rewarded.

Syed and Gladwell have articulated in their books what we all know as adults – you'll get nothing out of life if you don't work hard, aka Strummer's Law: no input, no output. The thing is, as a youth, I was the exception not the rule. I didn't mind beating golf balls all day

---

[1] Malcolm Gladwell, *Outliers: The Story of Success* (London: Penguin, 2009).

[2] Matthew Syed, *Bounce: The Myth of Talent and the Power of Practice* (London: Fourth Estate, 2011).

long. I loved spending hours on the putting green; indeed, when I came off my bike once and cut my hands all I could do for a week was putt, so I did, for ten hours a day. I can still putt better than 99.9% of the world's population.

One of my heroes as a youth was a South African golfer called Gary Player. He was an amazingly dedicated golfer. He practised like no other, mainly because he needed to; he had a mere grain of aptitude for the game and he knew he had to work harder than all the other golfers in order to make that grain grow.

One of Player's routines was to practise bunker shots until he holed out three times in a row – a fiendishly hard thing to do once, let alone three times. He won all four of golf's major championships. His name became synonymous with a single mantra, 'the harder I practice, the luckier I get'.

I wonder which green Gary Player was chipping onto when the Second World War broke out?

A growth mindset environment

> Growth is never by mere chance; it is the result of forces working together.
>
> James Cash Penney

In my experience, people behave according to your expectations. Back in 1999 I set up a media studies department at Huntington with the remarkable Karl Elwell, an Apple Distinguished Educator and colleague; we worked ridiculously hard. Not only did each of the gangster films we studied have its own separate notes page but each notes page was watermarked with the individual movie poster. Every minor detail was attended to at every level of the course.

Huntington School Sixth Form, Media Studies A2, Unit 4: Genre - The Heist Movie, 5 Wider Contexts

Film: The Killing (Kubrik, 1956)

Political:
- •
- •
- •
- •

Historical:
- •
- •
- •
- •

Economic:
- •
- •
- •
- •

Cultural:
- •
- •
- •
- •

Social:
- •
- •
- •
- •

One might argue that such elaborate effort was a waste of time, but that first cohort of A level students, whom we enveloped within our own wave of unbridled enthusiasm, worked as hard as we did. One of them admitted that when they saw how hard we were working, they felt they had no choice but to work equally hard. The vast majority of them went on to forge careers in the creative industries. (By the way, if you haven't seen Kubrik's *The Killing*, it's a cracking heist movie!)

I set out to exhibit in all aspects of my work the behaviours I would like to see replicated relentlessly, and this is key in helping to establish the school's culture. Importantly, I will challenge anyone who behaves in a way that is unaligned with the school's cultural tone.

I want to work in a school where industry and commitment are seen as cultural virtues by every member of the school community. Hardly remarkable, I know, but the opposite notion – getting rich quick with the minimum of effort – has plagued the human race for a long time. Go see Ben Jonson's *The Alchemist* if you don't believe me; I saw Sam Mendes' production at the Royal Shakespeare Company in the early 1990s and Sir Epicure Mammon was dressed in a banker's pin-striped suit. Jonson's play is the best explanation of why people still buy lottery tickets, even though if you buy a ticket on the Monday you've more chance of dying by the Saturday draw than winning the thing!

When it comes to success, and academic success in particular, there is no quick win. Telling a Year 10 lad, however, that they just need to work harder often doesn't help. Although I still feel as young and as excited about life as I did a quarter of a century ago, to any 14-year-old I look like a grey-haired old man going on and on and on. Trouble is, that's just what I am. I know what students need to do to be successful, but telling them to get their backsides in gear more often than not has the opposite effect.

If, however, instead of telling students to spend more hours working, you explain they have control over their brains and that they can change their attitude to work because they can change their mindset, you might just see them begin to work harder.

If you've been on Mars for the past two years, you may not have encountered Carol Dweck's work on developing a growth mindset.[3] Well, for the Martians amongst us, here's a summary of her thesis: Dweck claims, on the basis of good research, that people can choose what they think about their own intelligence. If you have a fixed mindset you see intelligence as unchangeable, you aim to present the image of being intelligent rather than being open to learning, and you avoid challenges because failing would see you lose your intelligent chimera. This rejection of challenge and learning prevents you from growing intellectually.

Conversely, if you view intelligence as something which can be developed, you have a growth mindset and you will put effort into strategies

---

3   See Dweck, *Mindset.*

that enhance learning and long-term successes. Dweck shows how it helps to encourage students to have a view of intelligence as something that can be developed. She does not deny that we all differ in our natural aptitudes but emphasises that our continued effort makes the most of our lot. Students with a growth mindset know that effort is the key to successful learning.

The thing that sets Dweck's growth mindset work apart from other popular fads in education – which, in fact, disqualifies it from being a fad at all – is that at its root is an eternal verity best captured in Tom Bennett's pithy conclusion to *Teacher Proof*: 'Carol Dweck's research falls into the category of most of the best of our research into education, in that it merely ends up confirming the eternal truths of the classroom: turn up, work hard, study, do well; work harder, do better; believe you can improve and you probably will, believe that you can't and see what happens.'[4]

The fact is, if you commit to something completely you almost certainly commit yourself to experiencing a degree of failure. On a profound level, any relationship you have will end, no matter how committed, because of the single certainty of the human condition. Students who commit to improving their performance at school will inevitably fail the majority of the time; it feels to me that too many learn that to avoid failure at school they can just refuse to commit. Changing their mindset and letting them understand that they have the power over how they think about studying is the nuanced approach to motivating students that growth mindset brings.

One of the great things about Dweck's work is how it makes you think. I had never thought through the psychology of how telling a student he is gifted is likely to have a detrimental effect on his commitment. According to Dweck, if a student is told he is gifted he will be less likely to work hard at something because, by definition, if he has to work at

---

[4] Tom Bennett, *Teacher Proof: Why Research In Education Doesn't Always Mean What It Claims, And What You Can Do About It* (London and New York: Routledge, 2013).

something, he is no longer naturally gifted – he's a worker like all the lesser mortals in his class.

I think Dweck's theory is spot on. However, just how do you systematically transform your school so that a growth mindset attitude runs through it like the words in a stick of seaside rock? The challenge for school leaders is to make real what Dweck (convincingly) theorises about attitudinal culture in schools – not an easy task.

It is important that you refine your approach to growth mindset as it becomes established. Initiatives can begin strongly then they diminish over time; they have a half-life, like nuclear material. We have come to realise that just working harder is never enough.

If you always do what you've always done, you'll always get what you've always got. This ubiquitous aphorism is such a cliché, but it is behind the conclusions drawn by Yeager, Walton and Cohen in their overview of research into the impact of growth mindset strategies in schools. They make the point that, 'When confronted with continued failures despite making more effort, students might conclude that they can't succeed, draining their motivation.'[5]

When I learnt how to play golf I practised for hours on end, but I always thought about the outcomes of my shots and I would change things if a fault crept into my game. And I always had a coach; I knew what I was doing, but I needed an expert to point out to me any subtle failings in my game which I hadn't identified.

What I had to prevent, during my endless hours of belting balls up the practice ground, was ingraining faults. The same applies to our students. Whilst the growth mindset emphasises the importance of hard work, the danger lies in dismaying students who work hard but don't improve, who keep doing what they have always done and get what they've always got. Yeager, Walton and Cohen's definition of growth

---

[5]   David Yeager, Gregory Walton and Geoffrey L. Cohen, Addressing Achievement Gaps With Psychological Interventions, *Kappan* 94(5) (2013): 62–65. Available at: https://web.stanford.edu/~gwalton/home/Welcome_files/ Yeager%20Walton%20Cohen%202013.pdf.

mindset development is a fuller formula for success: effort + strategies + help from others.

I write this at a time when the educational climate in England has become quite cold towards Sir Ken Robinson's vision of education; the backlash has begun. Robinson's most viewed ever TED talk shot him to fame, but now people are criticising his vision.[6] Joe Kirby goes as far as to say that 'Sir Ken is wrong on education: profoundly, spectacularly wrong.' He adds that, contrary to Sir Ken's view, 'Talent is not innate and that it's only dedicated, determined and disciplined practice that leads to great achievement.'[7]

I don't think Sir Ken has ever denied that disciplined practice is essential to great achievement. For instance, one of the case studies in *The Element* explains how world champion pool player Ewa Laurance, when she was 16, practised for ten or twelve hours every day, even bothering to get the key from the owner of the pool hall so she could play on her own before it opened.[8]

The Robinson/ Dweck innate talent/hard work dichotomy is a false one – I will happily champion both writers' views.

This much I know about developing a growth mindset culture

(This is an enhanced list compared to the others in the book.)

● Plan thoroughly the implementation of growth mindset for your specific school; you cannot launch growth mindset twice, so plan

---

[6] Ken Robinson, How Schools Kill Creativity [video], *TED* (February 2006). Available at: http://www.ted.com/talks/ken_robinson_says_schools_kill_creativity?language=en.

[7] Joe Kirby, What Sir Ken Got Wrong, *Pragmatic Education* (12 October 2013). Available at: http://pragmaticreform.wordpress.com/2013/10/12/what-sir-ken-got-wrong/.

[8] Robinson and Aronica, *The Element*.

hard before rolling it out. And think hard about what will work best at your school in your context. There are a number of schools now nurturing a growth mindset culture, and all the ones I know are, predictably, very keen to share their expertise.

- As Basil Fawlty once said, 'Special subject – the bleedin' obvious.' You cannot begin to think about developing a growth mindset in your school unless you have read the book and understand in a little more detail what Dweck is proclaiming.

- If you are serious about adopting the Dweck thesis, then make the development of a growth mindset culture a whole-school priority.

- You have to leap the cognitive hurdle first: convince your staff and then the students that intelligence is not fixed. It should be easy, shouldn't it? If intelligence *is* fixed we may as well all give up now. Convince the staff of the efficacy of the growth mindset. When you convince the staff, do three things: explain that brains can grow (the neuroscience bit), use hard data to show it works and emphasise to them that the whole project is about students working harder – the latter is a real winner. I think we are all tired of students' learnt helplessness.

- Convincing the students that they can all get better with effort hinges upon a really good explanation of the neuroscience. For many of our students the mere fact that their futures are not fixed is both revelatory and motivational. The Learning Pod's short video, *The Learning Brain*, is pretty good for engaging both students and teachers alike (as long as you ignore the brief allusion to visual, auditory and kinaesthetic (VAK) near the end).[9] If you want to read about the workings of our brains, you'll do no better than Andrew Curran's *The Little Book of Big Stuff About the Brain*.[10]

---

[9] Learning Curve Education [video], *The Learning Brain* (16 April 2010). Available at: http://www.youtube.com/watch?v=cgLYkV689s4.

[10] Andrew Curran, *The Little Book of Big Stuff About the Brain: The True Story of Your Amazing Brain* (Carmarthen: Crown House Publishing, 2008).

● Keep it simple. To begin with boil your approach down to something tangible for staff which is low cost and high impact. All 112 teachers at Huntington had one growth mindset strategy for our first year of growth mindset cultural development: whenever any student muttered the phrase, 'I can't do this', the teacher said, 'yet'; I have heard many of our students add the ubiquitous 'yet' when one of their peers has spouted the defeatist line.

● When you come to think about it, 'Work smarter, not harder' is unhelpful. It suggests there is a short cut to success. As an alternative, how about our line, 'Working harder makes me smarter'?

● In order to help you to evaluate the impact of your growth mindset culture, establish a hard data baseline. We used Dweck's own questionnaire for the students, and for the staff, Penny Hall, our subject leader science, developed our own. One of the development team grew up in a family where the single mantra was, 'There is no such thing as failure, just success and learning' – mum and dad helped with the questionnaire.

● You need to plan your testing systematically because once you know about growth mindset your mind will have already changed. Don't entitle the questionnaires 'Growth mindset questionnaire' or you'll get a *Cosmo*-style response. And, of course, there's always the Hawthorne effect, which suggests that the novelty of having research conducted, and the increased attention from it, could lead to temporary increases in productivity. This will skew your results if you are unnecessarily transparent about what the questionnaire is measuring.

● Dominic Cummings is unfairly dismissive of the Syed/Gladwell stance when he says, 'Various books have promoted the idea that people require the same amount of practice regardless of talent and that "10,000" hours is a sort of magic number – put in those hours and you too can be great, don't worry about your genes.'[11] What we

---

[11] Dominic Cummings, Some Thoughts on Education and Political Priorities, *The Guardian* (11 October 2013). Available at: http://www.theguardian.com/politics/interactive/2013/oct/11/dominic-cummings-michael-gove-thoughts-education-pdf.

are saying at Huntington is something more subtle: if you work hard then you can improve significantly, whatever your starting point. I will never be Jimi Hendrix, but if I really stuck at it I could improve my guitar playing considerably. To be fair to Cummings, his controversial treatise on the importance of genetics in children's academic careers is worth a read – it is much more nuanced than elements of the media may have led us to believe.

● We've come to the conclusion that gifted and talented is a dreadful label. We had a moment of illumination very recently. We asked ourselves, 'Why do we need such a label on our set lists?' And the answer is, of course, to help us ensure that our expectations of those particular students are appropriately high. Therefore, they are 'high starters': on our set lists we will have HS7, HS10 and HS12 for those students starting the key stage with high academic scores. If those high starters don't work hard they won't make the most of their aptitudes, and if you weren't a high starter at the start of the key stage then you can be by the time you start the next one.

● Once you start to think hard about what Dweck says you begin to question everything about what you do as a school leader. If Dweck is right – and in my personal experience I think she is – then setting students grades as targets is deeply flawed. The subject leaders of our two most successful A levels both fessed up to me that they don't look at students' targets. They don't consciously differentiate. They just teach to A* standard all of the time to all of the students. Go figure …

Chapter 12

You can't just wish to be better …

The learning game

> We all need people who will give us feedback. That's how we improve.
>
> **Bill Gates**

I began playing golf at about 8 or 9 years of age. To be good at golf, you have to get the basics right. Luckily for me, my dad sorted out my grip and my stance from the outset. He then gave me one piece of advice, 'effortless plays golf'. I didn't quite understand what he meant at first, but the more I played, the more I came to realise that, like any sport, golf is all about timing.

If you watch test cricket, you'll see a top-class batsman make what looks to be a gentle push forward with the bat, and the ball will hurtle off to the boundary, seemingly unstoppable. That's timing. The ball will have come out of the very centre of the bat, and every movement the batsman made to make that happen will have come together as one at the nano-second leather meets willow. The result is a seemingly effortless stroke of perfection. And four runs.

When I first saw top golf professionals play in the flesh, I was astounded at how slowly they swung the club. Simon Owen and Isao Aoki in the 1978 World Matchplay final at Wentworth had swings which were so slow they are probably still going on somewhere. The next day, back on the practice range, I was mimicking what I had seen the day before.

The best book I ever read about golf was Jack Nicklaus' *Golf My Way*.[1] One thing which struck me was Nicklaus' hands, prints of which appear in the centre of the book. When I was 14 it was good to know

---

[1]   Jack Nicklaus, *Golf My Way: The Instructional Classic* (New York: Simon & Schuster, 2005).

that, in terms of hand size at least, I had something in common with the best golfer in the world.

Trevor was the assistant professional at Piltdown and I caddied for him all over the country. It was great to watch him play and to be amongst great players. At the qualifying rounds for the 1980 British Open at Muirfield, I managed to spoof my way onto the Gullane No. 1 course for a practice round and rubbed shoulders with some stellar players. I watched a certain 14-year-old José María Olazábal, later to become US Masters champion and Ryder Cup captain, practise late into the evening on Gullane's village green.

In his book Nicklaus often refers to John Jacobs, one of the greatest ever golf coaches. Jacobs used to say that the best way to interpret what was happening with your golf swing was to study the flight of your ball when you hit a shot.[2] During the April of 1982 my shots were veering off short and to the right. It was the day before the Sussex under-18 championships and I had no real chance of successfully defending my title.

By that time John Amos was my golf coach. John was the professional at Piltdown, and he understood my game like no one else. He was a tall, imposing man of few words. I went to see him and we spent an hour together. We began with me hitting a dozen or so shots, most of which faded away short and right. He just watched.

Within five minutes John could see what was wrong. I had stopped getting a full shoulder turn and was just trying to pat the ball down the fairway. I was trying to *steer* the ball, rather than *hit* it. He repeated his favourite mantra about hitting the ball with the back of my left hand, and swung the club back for me whilst I continued to grip the club. Suddenly, with the help of my coach, I could realign my swing and hit the ball properly again. Hours of practice for the rest of the day to ingrain what John had taught me was all I needed; the next day, down on the Littlehampton links, I won the under 18 championship for the second time in succession.

---

[2] John Jacobs, *Golf in a Nutshell: The Flight of the Ball Tells It All* (London: Hodder & Stoughton, 1996).

So how did I learn how to play golf? I had a really good start with a patient, knowledgeable dad. I watched the very best players play. I played with people who were better than me. I read about the game. I practised hard. I was tested every weekend during the spring and summer when I competed in tournaments, and my scores were posted on the leader board for all to see. I was possessed with an unshakeable confidence.

One of my closest golfing mates was a bloke called Jamie Spence. We played together for Sussex several times. Once, when playing senior county golf, we recalled the day we had first met six years earlier at a schools' event when he had played horribly and I was runner-up to Paul Way. I said to Spence that all I could remember about him was that he liked the band Status Quo. He replied that his abiding memory of me was that I was a 'cocky bastard'. We were both right, but I'm not sure which one of us was more embarrassed.

The thing is, you can be as confident about your game as you like, practise as hard as you can, test yourself on the toughest courses against the best players, but if you do not have a great coach who gives you honest feedback, you'll never be a truly great golfer. No matter what the sport, all the best players have great coaches; all the best teams likewise. A truly great teacher makes all the difference.

Continuous professional development's golden thread

> We are what we repeatedly do. Excellence, then is not an act but a habit.
>
> Will Durant (and not Aristotle!)

Ultimately there can be no point in CPD for teachers if it does not impact upon learning.

Professor Rob Coe, in his inaugural lecture as director of the Centre for Evaluation and Monitoring and Professor of Education at the School of Education at the University of Durham, provided a devastating critique of the state of professional development in schools, concluding with four recommendations:

1   Get teaching really focused on learning.

2   Invest in effective professional development.

3   Use multiple sources of validated evidence to support diagnostic and constructive evaluation of teacher quality.

4   Whenever we make a change we must try to evaluate its impact as robustly as we can.[3]

Professor Coe finished his lecture with a challenge to all of us working in schools that are focused on improving the quality of teaching and learning: 'Education has existed in a pre-scientific world, where good measurement of anything important is rare and evaluation is done badly or not at all. It is time we established a more scientific approach.'[4] In Chapter 17, on the role of research in improving the quality of teaching and learning, I explore further how we might make teaching an evidence-based profession.

Not long ago I interviewed Alex Quigley for the post of director of research in teaching and learning at Huntington. His worst answer to the dozen or so questions I posed him was in response to this one: which CPD experience has had the most impact on your practice in the classroom? He thought about it for a bit, made a couple of false starts and eventually came up with something spurious and inconsequential. When we debriefed he admitted the question had stumped him because he could not genuinely think of a single moment in his career when formal CPD had impacted upon his teaching.

Alex is in the twelfth year of his career. I reckon that's 38 staff meetings, 60 training days and well over 100 department meetings without a single memorable worthwhile CPD experience. On one level that's pretty depressing, on another it's *completely* depressing when the fact is Alex has been at Huntington all that time.

---

3   Robert Coe, Improving Education: A Triumph of Hope Over Experience, inaugural lecture at Durham University, 18 June 2013. Available at: http://www. cem.org/attachments/publications/ImprovingEducation2013.pdf, pp. xiii–xvi.

4   Coe, Improving Education.

If it is so ineffectual, what is the point, then, of the vast majority of CPD in schools? What saves me from total despair at our CPD situation is that we now have a bottom-up approach to CPD. What we are doing is ensuring that we all have the space and time to work deliberately and continuously upon our practice and, having dispensed with attending expensive external courses which promise to move you to outstanding, we have confidence within ourselves to support each other to improve our teaching. As Tom Bennett said after Huntington hosted a researchED conference in May 2014, 'We need to get past the one-way, top down, all-at-once, all-at-the-start model of current practice. Get away from linear, paternalist paradigms where we passively receive the tablets from Moses.'[5]

What also saves me from total despair is that the person who wrote this about those expensive external courses:

You can argue such courses simply exaggerate their claims to sell their wares. This is likely true. 'Outstanding' gets plastered over a lot of CPD literature. You could argue that these programmes do no harm – that they spark reflection about practice, which is surely a good thing. Perhaps so, but a genuinely 'continuous' approach to teacher improvement, rooted in the daily practice of school-based training, is required and it would be more cost effective. Each and every school should define what great teaching is in their context and target all their CPD to this end. Sustained coaching, with a deep knowledge of the school context and the students, can help if it is part of a long-term process of improvement.[6]

– runs our CPD provision!

5   Tom Bennett, ResearchED York: It's Great Up North, *TES Connect* (5 May 2014). Available at: http://community.tes.co.uk/tom_bennett/b/weblog/archive/2014/05/03/researched-york-it-39-s-great-up-north.aspx.

6   Alex Quigley, 'Outstanding Teacher Programme' – Don't Believe the Hype, *Hunting English* (29 March 2014). Available at: http://www.huntingenglish.com/2014/03/29/outstanding-teacher-programme-dont-believe-hype/.

Whilst Alex Quigley is now shaping our CPD provision to ensure it meets the needs of as many individual teachers as possible, the relatively new element of our provision, which I want to write about in more detail, is our use of video observations to help teachers improve their teaching. However, the use of video technology to help colleagues improve their teaching has only been possible since we stopped grading individual lessons.

How do I know a teacher is a good teacher? Well, one thing is for certain, it's not by observing them teach in a formal, clipboard manner and grading individual lessons. If anyone involved in making formal judgements through lesson observations really thinks about it, the observation of the one-off performance lesson tells you nothing certain about the observed teacher's effectiveness.

One of our key policy changes at Huntington, which has had an inordinately positive impact upon our culture of improvement, is the decision not to grade individual lessons. Poor performance management systems, where the judgement of a teacher's overall effectiveness depends to a significant extent upon judgements of individual lessons, do nothing to improve the quality of teaching. Indeed, I would argue very strongly that such systems have the opposite effect: the teacher puts on a play-safe, performance lesson when observed and, once observed, doesn't think very hard at all about her pedagogy when no one is looking.

What I try to do in school is create a culture where what I observe in lessons is the same as what I would see if I was an unobtrusive fly on the wall in any random lesson, anywhere in the school and at any time of the year. If I can foster such a culture, then I can begin to help teachers improve their teaching at the margins of practice.

I know that many people have already argued that individual lessons shouldn't be graded,[7] but two things have recently brought home to us the folly of grading lessons. First, some of the vacuous reasons behind

---

[7] Amongst many contributions it is worth reading a post by Professor Rob Coe entitled, Classroom Observation: It's Harder Than You Think, *CEM Blog* (9 January 2014). Available at: http://www.cem.org/blog/414/.

judgements given by Ofsted inspectors during our last inspection: 'That was an Outstanding lesson up until the moment the students turned on the computers when the pace of their learning dipped a little so it can only be judged as Good.' I think the very average experience of our Ofsted inspection has given us both confidence and courage. And second, one of our performance development lesson observation debriefs began by the teacher saying to the deputy head teacher, 'Just give me the judgement: I've got lots of things to get on with.'

Graded judgements of individual lessons are unreliable and they get in the way of teachers working on their teaching skills, something even Ofsted has recognised – Mike Cladingbowl, the ex-national director for schools, said as much in his fascinatingly informal document, 'Why Do Ofsted Inspectors Observe Individual Lessons and How Do They Evaluate Teaching in Schools?'[8] If you haven't read Mike's thinking on the matter, it's well worth looking up. In September 2014 Ofsted made it clear that they will not grade individual lessons during inspection.[9]

The thing is, if we know that comment-only marking is best practice because it prevents students from just seeking the grade and ignoring constructive feedback for improvement, *the same has to be true for teachers.*

Now that we do not grade lesson observations, when it comes to performance management observations we can ask colleagues, 'How would you like to be observed to help you best develop your teaching?' That question alone changes the dynamic of the observation process. At first people responded quizzically to such a move, but since we made the decision to abandon making lesson judgements, the quality of conversations about improving teaching has risen beyond

---

[8]   Mike Cladingbowl, Why Do Ofsted Inspectors Observe Individual Lessons and How Do They Evaluate Teaching in Schools? (February 2014). Ref. 140050. Available at: http://dera.ioe.ac.uk/19361/.

[9]   Ofsted, Information for Teachers About the Inspection: Lesson Observations. Ref: 140102 (September 2014). Available at: http://dera.ioe.ac.uk/20770/1/ Information%20for%20teachers%20about%20inspection%20-%20lesson%20 observations.pdf.

expectation and the number of meaningful conversations about teaching has increased markedly. Teachers genuinely want to discuss their practice.

So, if you are in any doubt about why you should never grade lesson observations again, ask yourself this question: what do I add to my knowledge of the quality of teaching in our school by grading lessons? The answer, I am sure, will be nothing. Zilch. A big fat zero. Nowt as they say in Yorkshire. I know who teaches well in our school and I know the teachers who need some support in developing the effectiveness of their teaching.

Since we have stopped grading individual lessons we have made performance management a genuinely effective vehicle for growing great teachers. I line manage directly thirty teachers; my responsibility as performance management reviewer to those colleagues is as important as any of my responsibilities as head teacher. If I can get the process right I reckon I will, as a performance management reviewer, have a huge impact on student outcomes.

In these times of austerity all our resources need to be directed towards improving teaching. I spend 150 hours observing lessons in a year and the £8,000 the hours cost the school need to equate to £8,000 of positive impact upon those colleagues' teaching skills. Time is our most precious and limited resource; it seems madness to spend so much time in classrooms without that investment in my time helping to improve significantly the quality of teaching at Huntington.

Graham Nuthall's *The Hidden Lives of Learners* is one of the best books I have read on teaching and learning. It unveils beautifully the complexities of the learning process. He identifies three lives of learners in the classroom: the life which appears to be happening between the teacher and the students, the life of learning which occurs between students and the third life – the one that happens inside their heads. Nuthall's book reveals how meaningful research into teaching and learning requires use of audio-visual technologies and painstaking analysis. The use of video and good sound recording is an important addition to improving teaching in schools.

In my experience, without a video record of the lesson, the developmental potential of the lesson observation process can never be fully realised. When Jonathan Raban was writing his travel book *Coasting*,[10] he met Paul Theroux in Brighton who was writing his own book, *The Kingdom by the Sea*.[11] The meeting features in both books, and this is Raban's reflections upon Theroux's account of their meeting:

> His book, *The Kingdom by the Sea*, came out a year later, in 1983. I read it avidly and with mounting anxiety. It had only one seriously flat patch, I thought – his account of our meeting in Brighton. There wasn't a single start of recognition for me in his two pages: what he described was not at all what I remembered. But then memory, as Paul had demonstrated ... is a great maker of fictions.[12]

My experience of certain post-observation discussions has been similar, and I wager there have been individual colleagues who thought that my account of their lesson was not at all what they remembered. I recall discussing a lesson once where the teacher could not recollect what he had said and only reluctantly accepted my version of events because I had written down what he had said verbatim.

Teachers are often reluctant to be filmed teaching because they think it will be used against them in the performance management process should the lesson prove a disaster. Once that fear is removed – because the process is not *management* but *development* and pay award decisions are not based upon the grade judgement of an individual lesson – teachers are much more inclined to be filmed. If the purpose of lesson observations is to grow teachers, not grade them, you will be amazed at how open colleagues are to filming themselves teaching.

Once the fear of being filmed has been removed, there is a second hurdle to o'erleap – the embarrassment of watching yourself on screen. The solution to the second hurdle is to encourage colleagues to film

---

[10] Jonathan Raban, *Coasting* (London: Picador, 1985).

[11] Paul Theroux, *The Kingdom by the Sea* (London: Penguin, 1985).

[12] Raban, *Coasting*.

themselves first to gain confidence. Once they have got over the shock of seeing and hearing themselves, ask them to share their video with you when they are ready so you can coach them, but not a moment before they are ready.

Working on my own coaching feedback has taken enormous effort. I have spent the last two years working on just three aspects of my practice: my body language, my tone of voice when asking questions and my language of praise. It's hard work. I have felt compelled to persevere for two reasons: first because improving at the margins of my practice will benefit my students and they will learn more effectively. The second reason lies at the heart of why I think a head teacher should be the head *teacher*: it's because I want every single teacher at Huntington to work on their own teaching in a similar way. In the end, I cannot expect the teachers I employ to be committed to making continuous marginal improvements in their teaching if I just churn out thoughtless, ill-planned lessons and never worry about getting any better as a teacher.

Here's what I'm working on at the moment: I'm fascinated to figure out whether it is possible to ask a student a question without giving some sort of subliminal clue as to the answer. My quest derives from being observed: in feedback, my observers remarked how my body language explicitly guided the students towards the answer.

Good observers see the things that you don't see or choose not to see. When I was questioning, I was sort of conscious that I was guiding students to an answer on a subliminal level. As I asked Joe, 'If income tax is reduced, is that likely to increase or decrease consumer spending?' I could feel my outstretched hand rise up. It was funny, but I couldn't stop it. In my marginal anxiety for Joe and the rest of the group to give a good response, my body language was providing them with the answer rather than developing their thinking and their learning more effectively. And this is just what the two observers fed back to me. So, armed with our new specialist lesson observation video equipment, I filmed myself teach.

Video technology has come a long way since the static VHS at the back of the classroom. I remember years ago filming myself teaching in a cramped room with one narrow walkway between the two columns of chairs. The clunky VHS camera was perched on the top of the filing cabinet at the far end of the room. The only thing I remember about the video – and I mean the *only* thing – was how I walked down the class between the columns of students with a hand on each of my buttocks. Bizarre stuff. Now I have to get over the middle-aged, grey-haired, slightly portly imposter with the Jimmy Hill chin who happens to be me.

My self-analysis has helped me with my questioning and body language significantly. Having watched myself teach for many hours now, and shared the videos with a teacher-coach from the drama department, I have learnt how to plan questions far more precisely before I ask them and to control consciously my body language. Keeping focused on the small developmental area of my practice between coaching sessions requires real discipline. However, through my own hard work the quality of discussion in my economics lessons has improved significantly, and the students' confidence has grown purely because I have consciously developed my practice.

On occasion I experiment with my teaching skills mid-lesson. In a recent lesson I asked Harry, a Year 12 student, a question about whether a reduction in the rate of interest was likely to increase aggregate demand. I wanted to see whether I could ask the question in such a deadpan way that I gave no clue when asking the question and, most importantly, during the string of follow-up questions, as to whether his answer was on the right track or not.

After his initial response that there would be an increase in aggregate demand, I asked Harry, without any clues in my body language and in a completely toneless voice, 'How do you know?' Now, Harry's a confident lad, but he suddenly looked confused and the colour drained from his face. His reply was a mutter. When we'd finished, we deconstructed what had happened and he said that my featureless questioning had really disconcerted him. We concluded that in twelve years of education he had got used to the subliminal messages of encouragement that emanate from a teacher when interacting with a student.

Progress is spiky for all learners. In the same way that we understand that students do not make linear progress, so it is for me and my teaching. However, since I began working on my body language and questioning I have been much more controlled in these aspects of my teaching and much more deliberate. I haven't suddenly become a robot but I consciously mediate my normally enthusiastic body language. I consider posting my videos on my blog and then email the link to all staff for my colleagues to watch. It is an important element of leading teaching and learning at Huntington. It's integral to being the head *teacher*.

I think the one person who has illustrated what it really takes to improve your teaching more than any other is Doug Lemov. His book *Teach Like a Champion* is evidence, if ever it were needed, that many teaching techniques are learnable and that good teaching is not a gift – it is something which we can all learn; moreover, we can all learn to improve our teaching.[13] What is remarkable is the partner publication, the *Field Guide*, which takes you through exactly how you might develop a certain teaching skill.[14] Its rigorously detailed, step-by-tiny-step walk-throughs of how to work by yourself on very specific elements of your practice are hugely useful to give to individual colleagues to support their quest to become better teachers.

I watched a recording of a lesson recently with the teacher and she was stunned by how many students were not listening to her, even though she thought they were all paying attention when she was explaining a crucial learning point. Two things to note from this experience: first, the incredible usefulness of recorded observations for allowing colleagues to see for themselves how they might improve at the margins of their practice. Second, there is a section in Lemov's book

---

[13] Doug Lemov, *Teach Like a Champion: 49 Techniques That Put Students on the Path to College* (San Francisco, CA: Jossey-Bass, 2010).

[14] Doug Lemov, *Teach Like a Champion Field Guide: A Practical Resource to Make the 49 Techniques Your Own* [inc. DVD] (San Francisco, CA: Jossey-Bass, 2012).

called '100 Percent' – 'the *one* suitable percentage of students following a direction given in your classroom'[15] – and since watching the recording the teacher has been using the corresponding chapter from the *Field Guide* to help her ensure that all her students are attentive when she is speaking.

With good teachers you're working at the margins of skill development. At the moment I am working with a number of colleagues on very specific elements of their practice: tone of voice, gestures, questioning, the language of growth mindset and the deployment of teaching assistants. And for these good teachers, it will take tremendous conscious effort to change practice that has been ingrained for years. It's Doug Lemov stuff – working on marginal elements of your teaching requires fully conscious effort.

Doug Lemov cites Joshua Foer – from the latter's study of memory, *Moonwalking with Einstein*[16] – when discussing how teachers improve their own practice: 'The secret to improving at a skill is to retain some degree of conscious control over it while practising ... to force oneself to stay out of autopilot.' Lemov goes on to say, 'The process of intentionally implementing feedback is likely to keep people in a practice state of increased consciousness and thus steeper improvement.'[17]

Unsurprisingly, when it comes to improving teaching, our lesson observation camera is becoming one of the most important bits of kit in our school; there's always something to learn when you watch yourself teach. However, whilst we have all, at some time or another, intended to work on the feedback given to us about our teaching, as Lemov says, 'we end up losing sight of it amidst the wreckage of our tasks list'. Or perhaps we try it briefly and tell ourselves we have made

---

[15] Lemov, *Teach Like a Champion*.

[16] Joshua Foer, *Moonwalking with Einstein: The Art and Science of Remembering Everything* (New York: Penguin, 2011).

[17] Doug Lemov, Exclusive Excerpt: Doug Lemov's 'Practice Perfect', *Chalkbeat New York* (9 October 2012). Available at http://ny.chalkbeat.org/2012/10/09/exclusive-excerpt-doug-lemovs-practice-perfect/.

enough progress, or that the feedback wouldn't really work.'[18] The school culture has to prioritise professional development if the quality of teaching across a school is going to be comprehensively great.

If developing practice is not privileged within a school it is very hard to engage teachers in meaningful development of their own teaching. Zoë Elder is spot on when she says in her brilliant book, *Full On Learning*, 'Working in a climate of reflective practice is a vital strand of great professional development, especially when it is integrated as a systematic, school-wide, cultural approach to teaching and learning.'[19]

What we have done at Huntington is focus increasingly upon the only thing that matters – improving systematically the quality of teaching. I once asked an interviewee about his professional development needs. His reply was about something quite tangential to teaching, so I then asked whether he thought he had cracked this teaching thing. Post-interview my colleague remarked that I had been hard on the candidate with my testy response, 'because not many schools are as explicitly concerned as ours with improving our teaching'.

As our school grows in confidence we aim to introduce an Open Gardens-style initiative, where subject areas open up their class-rooms for a week to show their colleagues their best teaching. I think our decision to stop grading lessons is a major step to realising the school culture I have always idealised – a place, as Barth envisaged, 'that accord[s] a special place to philosophers who constantly examine and question and frequently replace embedded practices by asking "why" questions.'[20]

So much for Robinson, Barth, Lemov, et al. When it comes to teacher development, there are a few people closer to home who I think are worth listening to. Shaun Allison, in his superb book on the matter, defines precisely what teachers need if they are going to improve their practice: 'We need to give staff a range of CPD opportunities that will

---

[18] Lemov, Exclusive Excerpt: Doug Lemov's 'Practice Perfect'.

[19] Zoë Elder, *Full On Learning* (Carmarthen: Crown House Publishing, 2012).

[20] Barth, *Improving Schools from Within*.

engage, enthuse and motivate them. By this ... I mean a rich and varied ongoing programme of activities that staff can engage with on a number of levels and which will support them to reflect upon and develop their own practice.'[21] Shaun's book is an excellent compendium of advice and activities which I would recommend to any head teacher who wants to improve the effectiveness of her school's CPD provision.

The Teacher Development Trust, led by its inspirational CEO David Weston, provides the best support for school-based CPD I know.[22] David talks such great sense when it comes to CPD: 'The research evidence is clear that the most important action that schools can take to improve outcomes for students is supporting their teachers to be more effective, and the most reliable way to achieve this is to develop a professional culture where teachers are continually adapting and refining their skills and methods.'[23]

Weston's team provides members of his National Teacher Enquiry Network (NTEN) with a comprehensive package of measures which help schools to review their current CPD provision and then tailor a revised model of provision to meet the specific CPD needs of their teachers. As a member of NTEN we have connections with a whole range of like-minded schools working hard to provide CPD which is impactful.

The TeachMeet initiative is, perhaps, where the future of school improvement lies. I really do not know where the TeachMeet thing originated, but the likes of Ross Morrison McGill, Stephen Lockyer, Hélène Galdin-O'Shea, Keven Bartle and Kenny Pieper (Kenny is the inspiration behind Pedagoo[24]) have had a lot to do with its growth over the last two years. It seems to me that the TeachMeet scene has

---

21 Shaun Allison, *Perfect Teacher-Led CPD* (Carmarthen: Independent Thinking Press, 2014).

22 See http://www.teacherdevelopmenttrust.org/.

23 See http://tdtrust.org/our-work-2/evidence/.

24 See http://www.pedagoo.org/.

the energy of the most interested practitioners magnified ten-fold through collaboration.

As I have already pointed out, ideas in teaching are often disseminated using a top-down model. We need a bottom-up model of joint practice which finds solutions through collaborative working. The synergy of Twitter–blogging–CPD is so powerful. I think it is at the heart of facilitating the bottom-up approach to improving classroom practice. On reflection, TeachMeets might just be the response of the profession to spending cuts in schools.

As we anticipate further funding cuts in education through to 2020 we will have to be even more prudent. Lord Nash is on record as saying, 'Given the state of the public finances we have inherited, this government has done pretty well to protect the schools budget, but I'm afraid that whichever party wins the 2015 election there will be further cuts in the public sector.'[25]

Often, in austere times, head teachers cut the one thing they absolutely cannot afford to cut – CPD provision. I would argue that the CPD budget is the *one* budget that head teachers should protect above all others. One could go as far as to claim that our students' futures depend upon the ability of school leaders to develop truly great teachers – it's the golden thread.

This much I know about how you can't just wish to be better

- If you want all your colleagues to keep trying to improve their teaching at the margins, you have to create the conditions in your school for that to happen – focus every system on improving teaching.

---

[25] Lord Nash quoted in Nick Morrison, Schools Face Post-Election Funding Squeeze, Warns Minister, TES (11 October 2014). Available at: https://news. tes.co.uk/b/news/2014/10/10/schools-face-funding-squeeze-warns-minister. aspx.

- Assume everyone wants to improve their work and talk relentlessly as though that is happening across the school.

- Let your best teachers influence significantly your teacher improvement systems.

- Protect your CPD budget at all costs.

- Bottom-up wins every time when it comes to CPD.

Chapter 13

Developing *not managing* people

Work experience

> My brother always said you'd have to be mad to be a football manager. What other job is there where your entire livelihood depends on 11 daft lads?
>
> Francis Lee

Francis Lee played football for Manchester City. He was a prolific goal scorer and a genuine character; he played at a time when the only diet for footballers was of the 'see food and eat it' variety.

Lee began his football career with Bolton Wanderers. He then joined Manchester City and he also played for England. As a teenager at Bolton, Lee supplemented his income by driving an old brewery lorry to collect wastepaper. He spotted a market for toilet tissue and invested his earnings from football into his business. He sold the company in 1984 for £8.35 million. In 1994 he returned to buy a significant stake in Manchester City which he sold in 2007, making £6 million.

Lee was clearly an astute man. His entrepreneurship should be lauded. When he became the chairman of Manchester City in 1994 my friend, David Conn, interviewed him about the future of the club. It took David twenty minutes before he realised that all Lee was talking about was the number of restaurants he envisaged in the club's proposed new stadium. The thing is, unlike Lee, I can never imagine working for the money alone.

When I left school at 16 to try to make it as a golf professional, I had a number of part-time jobs. To begin with I worked for my girlfriend's dad, Tony Sutton, painting and decorating. There are some shoddily decorated houses down in the south-east corner of England as a result of my brief encounter with a paintbrush. Creosoting the underside eaves of a hotel roof was pretty grim: no overalls, no mask and no clue what I was doing. The brown caustic muck ended up in my eyes, up my nose and in my mouth.

At least Tony was decent to me. The most enlightening and frightening job I had was cleaning cars at a repair garage. I was battered. I was sent for tartan paint and all those other teases which befall any junior in such a macho world; worse, however, was the official welcome to the garage. They had a huge gantry which would be positioned over the bonnet so that the engine could be chained up and out of the car. The initiation ceremony entailed hauling me up on the gantry chains, stripping my trousers off and threatening to spray Schutz, the asphalt-based underbody sealant, all over my crotch. I'd forgotten the strategies I'd learnt in dealing with the council estate toughs at primary school and the more I struggled, the more fun they had. It was truly terrifying.

What I learnt was what monotonous manual work can do to people. Hauling me up in the gantry was the entertainment which punctuated another otherwise forgettable day. Another time they pushed me into the space for the spare coffin underneath the plinth in a hearse we were repairing. Oh, how they laughed.

Grown men were reduced to puerile games. I remember one lunchtime when the panel beaters at the garage had placed the tallest ladder they could find against the wall and were seeing who could climb to the highest rung. When they asked me to have a go I arrogantly dismissed it as childish, for which I got a whack from Martin, one of the younger men. I shudder now to think I was so patronising.

At one point I worked as an administrative assistant in the treasury department at County Hall. It was cleaner than the garage but just as tedious. One of my responsibilities was, ironically, to file the free school meal returns from schools across East Sussex. There were boxfuls of the things and I know for sure that no one ever looked at them.

I took away two things from my initial experience of work. First, that I could never endure such monotony; fortunately, I had a choice, because I had decent enough academic qualifications which meant that if my golfing ambitions came to naught, I could return to education. And second, that I had to find something to do in life which had some meaning; I needed to live to work as well as work to live.

Even if I had made it as a professional, in some ways I think a golf career would have been disappointing. It would have been easy to have been good but not quite good enough and to have lived a life half-fulfilled on featureless practice grounds and in faceless hotel rooms across Europe.

Reflecting now, teaching was the obvious career. It is selfless and the pleasure is in seeing others thrive. I genuinely love my job. In the end, being a head teacher has helped me to realise my ultimate aim in life: namely, to leave the world a slightly better place for my having been there. Ultimately, it is about developing every single child in your care.

It's development, stupid!

What we want for our students we should want for our teachers: learning, challenge, support, and respect.

Andy Hargreaves

When thinking about the systems to drive the improvement of teaching and learning, we returned to Huntington's three values – respect, honesty, kindness – and used them as the anvil upon which we forged our new performance management policy. If you can nail down your performance management policy, your pay policy also follows on naturally – something you have to draw up in this era of performance-related pay and which needs to be entirely aligned with your cultural norms.

Up until this point I have used the term 'performance management'. However, we call our performance management policy our 'performance *development* policy', and certainly would never use the word 'appraisal'. The word 'development' signifies to all our staff the tone of our approach to appraisal, and I will use this term from now on.

Consistency is the key to making fair judgements about the performance of your teachers. Three years ago we decided that the eight core members of the SLT would be responsible for the whole performance development process, even though we have as many as 112 teachers. This removed the responsibility from subject leaders in line with our drive to support them with their main role of growing great teachers, and it has enabled them to focus on professionally developing their teams.

It is very hard to be poacher and gamekeeper. Some subject leaders are close friends of those colleagues whose performance development reviews they undertake; asking the hard questions is difficult, if not impossible. One colleague head teacher accused me of emasculating our subject leaders, but I couldn't agree. Three years on, some head teachers are looking around for ways to ensure the rigour and consistency in their appraisal process that we have established in our performance development system.

At the moment we use the Teachers' Standards as the nominal benchmark against which to come to a judgement about the performance of teachers.[1] However, we are currently working on a new policy which will use our beloved 'Features of Truly Great Teaching' instead (see Chapter 1); the change will bring even greater coherence to our systems.

When setting performance development objectives, teachers should identify areas for development against the Teachers' Standards – or whichever benchmark might be used – as the focus for their objectives. At Huntington, meeting the objectives is not a prerequisite for a teacher's successful annual review of performance. I'll write that again: at Huntington, meeting the objectives is not a prerequisite for a teacher's successful annual review of performance.

If you do make meeting the objectives a prerequisite for a successful review then you will blunt any teacher's ambition to become a better

---

[1] Department for Education, Teachers' Standards, 1 July 2011 (introduction updated June 2013). Available at: https://www.gov.uk/government/collections/teachers-standards.

teacher. Why take the risk of setting yourself an ambitious development objective if your next pay award decision depends upon it? Think of your best teachers. They could set themselves objectives which would elevate them from truly great to god-like, never meet the objectives but still remain your best teachers, and be judged remarkable against the Teachers' Standards. Are you going to deny them a pay award for not meeting their hugely challenging objectives?

Our judgement of the performance of our teachers is based upon their performance against the Teachers' Standards. At the annual review meeting, the teacher provides the following mandatory evidence:

- Review of her students' examination results against the students' academic targets, providing class-by-class commentary on their students' performance.

- Lesson observation feedback.

- The teacher's 'Growing Great Teachers Professional Development Journal/Blog' (see below) as a record of her reflections upon her development as a teacher over the year.

- Feedback from work scrutinies.

- Good evidence of thoughtful lesson planning.

- Any further evidence which might relate specifically to the teacher's performance development objectives.

The teacher is welcome to provide any other evidence which will exemplify her performance against the Teachers' Standards. The mandatory evidence required should be sufficient enough to allow the SLT reviewer to make a well-informed judgement of the teacher's performance against the Teachers' Standards; the evidence should derive naturally from the school's/teacher's core self-evaluation processes and the teacher's professional obligation to continuously improve her practice.

An important element of our mandatory evidence is a 'Growing Great Teachers Professional Development Journal' where teachers keep a record of exactly how they are working on their teaching as part of their professional obligation to improve their practice. This keeps the relationship between teacher autonomy and accountability in fruitful balance.

We think it is important to be clear about our expectations of student performance at Huntington without trying to pin down student examination outcomes to fixed percentages. We have a general statement about our high expectations:

The following statement is designed to clarify what is expected of Huntington School teachers so that:

- There is no doubt about the level of performance required by our teachers.

- The need to reduce performance measures to overly specific and inflexible numerical targets is obviated.

It is a given that the assessment of a teacher's performance during the performance development review meeting will be rooted in the mandatory evidence. However, it is important to be clear that the final judgement of a teacher's performance on our 1–5 grading system will be made within the context of our school, where, historically:

- Students enter the school at attainment levels above the national average.

- Students make progress above the expected progress nationally.

- Students leave at the end of Key Stage 4 and Key Stage 5 with attainment levels above the national average.

- Teachers have the highest expectations of all our students, reflected in our growth mindset culture.

Judgements will be made with professional wisdom and will take into account a teacher's contextual analysis of the academic performance of students in his/her individual classes.

It is also important to acknowledge that the school development plan has explicitly high expectations of the quality of teaching at our school, with the ambition that 60% of the teaching in our school will be judged truly great and 40% judged good.

The professional judgement of reviewers will be central to making judgements about teacher performance. To that end, the SLT members who undertake all performance development assessments at Huntington are well-trained and the consistency of their judgements is maintained through systematic moderation procedures, which include the moderation of objective setting and judging evidence against the Teachers' Standards and observation of performance development review conversations. Although it might never be perfect, without being excessive these activities help to ensure a high level of consistency.

We didn't spend hours of our lives devising a gradated grid of each Teachers' Standard and sub-standard with descriptors of exceeding/ met/nearly met/not met; you will still have to use your professional judgement as there will always be circumstances for which your grid doesn't quite cater. When you begin trying to pin down gradated descriptors the meanings of words begin to blur.

It is important that your performance development annual cycle is not seen as a September-to-September process and between those two moments never the reviewer and the teacher shall meet. We have a cycle symbolised by an old-fashioned telephone wire whereby reviewer and teacher meet several times a year to ensure that the teacher is supported through the performance development process and that the development of their practice is continuous (as shown overleaf).

One of the challenges in schools is to ensure that we do not duplicate effort. A school's performance development processes should drive the improvement of teaching coherently through its CPD provision. If you can get your performance development process right then the link to CPD and improving the quality of teaching will be quite natural: conversely, get your performance development processes wrong and your efforts to improve the quality of teaching will be strangled at birth.

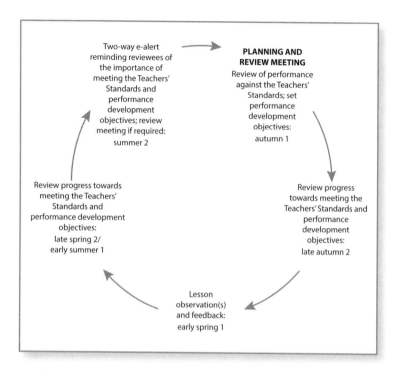

A final word about developing people within the new world of performance-related pay: trust your governing body and they will trust you. When I began as a head teacher, I thought I had to shoulder all the responsibility of leading a school. What I know now is that your governing body is an incredibly valuable resource. Governors should be critical friends, holding you to account and supporting you in equal measure. If anyone reading this book is a head teacher, or aspires to be a head teacher, be sure to tell your governing body everything: it helps you sleep at night if you've nothing whatsoever to hide.

This much I know about developing not managing people

- Accountability and development can go hand in hand if you create a values-driven school.

- Whatever you like to call it, appraisal has to be an integral part of professional development, not separate or bolt-on.

- Design coherent processes so there isn't a hint of repetition in your institution's systems.

- Love the one you're with – if your professional development processes are effective they'll morph into the one you love.

- If you ever have to move to capability procedures, do it with the utmost humanity.

Chapter 14

It's not about the money

Growing up

> We get bigger, taller, older. But, for the most part, we're still a bunch of kids, running around the playground, trying to fit in.
>
> Meredith Grey, Grey's Anatomy

Growing up is a tricky business. I never really wanted to be an adult. Even when I was at university I could never imagine getting a proper job. I couldn't conceive of having enough money to own a house. I certainly couldn't envisage having children.

When I was really young I did have this vague notion that earning £100 a week would mean I had really and truly made it. £100 was a fantastical sum of money, a figure that seemed to me way beyond anything anybody I knew was earning. Even when mother inherited tens of thousands of pounds it didn't really change things – her thriftiness was in her very veins and even now, at the age of 79, I have to push her to spend anything.

When I was a car cleaner in 1980 I earned £1.25 an hour; I even had to haggle with the boss to secure the extra twenty-five pence. The pecuniary reward for working in the council's treasury department was pretty meagre. Greenkeeping felt much more lucrative at £3 an hour which, for casual labouring in the mid-1980s, was a decent rate of pay.

When I made it to university I lived on a full non-repayable grant and tuition fees were unimaginable. Geoff Wall, my personal tutor, told us that we should feel scandalised because our maintenance grants had been cut by 20% in the twelve years since he had been an undergraduate. Despite what Geoff said, I remember walking out of the dining hall in Vanbrugh College on 10 October 1984 with my £630 termly grant cheque feeling like the richest man in the northern hemisphere. It was unheard of wealth as far as I was concerned.

When it came to accommodation, I was allocated room C203b, a split-double room in Vanbrugh College. A split-double is a double room which has had a corridor driven through its middle to create, on either side, two single rooms of the narrowest proportions. I couldn't open my door fully as it jammed against the single bed which was pushed hard against the far wall; spartan wasn't the word for it. The toilet was down the corridor, with toilet paper of the tracing paper variety which seemed functionally useless. The shower was next door to the toilet.

When I finished university in 1987 I came away with the smallest of overdrafts, and that was despite collecting the whole of the 1986 World Cup Panini sticker album which, if you have ever done such a thing, costs about as much as a two-bedroomed flat in Knightsbridge.

The state had invested in me. I was a model of social mobility. Thinking about it, another motivation for me to teach was, perhaps, some sense of wanting to give something back for what I had received. For me, teaching was one of the most respected, socially purposeful professions, even if it wasn't well-paid.

I teach economics A level and when I explain interest rates one of the things I impress upon my students is the current six-year record low Bank of England base rate of 0.5%. I show a graph which illustrates the history of the base rate going back centuries. I always point out that the base rate was at its zenith of 16% in 1988, the very year Louise and I bought our first flat.

My starting salary as a teacher at Eastbourne Sixth Form College was £8,859. The figure is ingrained in my memory. Louise was undertaking a PGCE and we depended, essentially, upon my salary. I brought home £515 per month and our mortgage on a one-bedroomed ground floor flat in a converted terraced house just off the Lewes Road was £345 per month.

When the 1991 recession hit the UK we were paying £345 per month in mortgage payments for a flat which cost £44,000 and was suddenly worth £25,000. We added the term 'negative equity' to our vocabulary. Like I said, I never really wanted to be an adult and I especially didn't want to be an adult in 1991.

I now earn hugely more than £26,000, the national average salary in the UK, and I feel well-remunerated for my job. That said, I'm not always sure what kind of salary such a job should attract, for it's not always good to think about the responsibility that being the head teacher of a large comprehensive school entails. When I was explaining to my son what I do, I compared it to being a parent to 1,500 students for nine hours every day.

Ultimately, 1,500 sets of parents entrust their most precious possession to my care; I sometimes think that my biggest daily responsibility is not to educate the students at Huntington School but to make sure they get home safely. It's certainly a surprising job for someone who once couldn't imagine ever being a parent.

What drives me above all else, however, is ensuring that our students have the best chance possible of improving their lot, that they do not limit themselves by their own perception of what they might achieve in life and that they have a choice about their career path. Whilst it's not about the money as far as I am concerned, it is, to a significant extent, about my students' lifelong earning potential.

Thinking through performance-related pay

> For people who don't know where their next meal is coming, notions of finding inner motivation are comical.
>
> Daniel Pink

Warning! Being idealistic about pay, when you are well-paid, is dangerous. What follows implicitly acknowledges that most teachers in England are paid pretty well and that if you stay in the profession long enough you'll earn way above the average annual salary in this country. Work in a car repair garage or as a painter and decorator, and what you are paid becomes much more important.

Daniel Pink's *Drive* illustrates with some style just why performance-related pay is such a wrong-headed policy for a school.[1] Most professionals, Pink claims, are motivated by the drive for autonomy, mastery and purpose – a triumvirate which is perfect for the teaching profession.

W. Edwards Deming felt similarly to Pink, in that he saw performance-related rewards in a negative light. Number twelve of Deming's fourteen points for the effective management of an organisation was, '*Remove barriers that rob people … of their right to pride of workmanship.* This means, inter alia, abolishment of the annual or merit rating and of management by objectives.'[2] All Deming wanted his employees to obsess about was the quality of their work, to be as good as they could possibly be and not to be distracted by competing against colleagues for salary increments.

What follows are my thoughts on performance-related pay, a policy made mandatory by legislation and which schools now have to implement.

To begin with, I didn't go into education to make money and I don't know any teacher who did. My profit is great examination results for our students. That's what I'm required to provide and that is what motivates me.

It is possible to pare my job down to one thing: to ensure that £7.5 million a year is spent in a way which provides the best education possible for the students who attract the money in the first place. Consequently, I cannot afford to reward poor teaching and never have done. It follows, then, that highly effective performance development mechanisms negate the need for performance-related pay.

If a teacher really isn't performing well, and all support mechanisms have been exhausted, they should be facing capability procedures in a

---

[1] Daniel Pink, *Drive: The Surprising Truth About What Motivates Us* (New York: Riverhead Books, 2011).

[2] Deming, *Out of the Crisis*, quoted in Crawford et al., *The School for Quality Learning*.

fair and transparent way. Everyone else should be developing their practice and performing well in the classroom.

Singling out teacher effectiveness as the variable solely responsible for student outcomes is a hugely complex business and way beyond the scope of even the best performance-related pay policy for teachers. Indeed, the Sutton Trust's *Improving the Impact of Teachers on Pupil Achievement in the UK* cites overwhelming evidence which shows that 'there is almost no link between teachers' prior education or experience and the achievement of their pupils.'[3] Steve Munby told the Association of School and College Leaders conference in 2012 that, 'If you are the longest serving head teacher in the hall you're probably our best or our worst head teacher.'[4] Like I said, judging teacher effectiveness is complex.

Attempts to make judgements about pay progression completely objective verge on the impossible. I've heard of one model where there are four elements which combine to provide an impartial numeric measure for making the pay progression decision: the grade for lesson observation 1; the grade for lesson observation 2; the quality of marking and assessment gleaned from a work scrutiny; and student examination data. Each element constitutes 25% of the final figure which determines the decision, and if the teacher gets 70% or above he progresses up the pay scale. An outstanding observation grade gains a full 25%, a good observation grade 17.5% … yes, it's mad isn't it? And it's still based on a number of relatively subjective judgements!

Performance-related pay induces competitiveness right down to the teacher-to-teacher level: why share my teaching resources with him if his students' results improve and he will get a pay rise over me? Fullan and Hargreaves point out, 'Trust and expertise work hand in hand to

[3] Sutton Trust, *Improving the Impact of Teachers on Pupil Achievement in the UK – Interim Findings* (September 2011). Available at: http://www.suttontrust.com/ researcharchive/improving-impact-teachers-pupil-achievement-uk-interim-findings/.

[4] Steve Munby, keynote speech at the annual conference of the Association of School and College Leaders, Birmingham, 23–24 March 2012.

produce better results … social capital strategies are one of the cornerstones for transforming the profession. Behaviour is shaped by groups much more than by individuals … if you want positive change, then get the group to do the positive things that will achieve it.'[5]

In schools where performance-related pay is rigidly enforced, where wisdom and judgement amongst the leadership team have vanished, who wants to teach set 4 out of 5? The more you think about performance-related pay, the more the intricacies emerge. How will re-setting mid-year affect pay progression decisions? Timetabling difficulties mean you have to take on a Year 11 group in September – are you then held responsible for that group's outcomes?

As Fullan says, 'Never a tick box, always complexity.'[6] The reason the School Teachers' Pay and Conditions Document (STPCD) is a weighty tome is because how you pay people is a complex issue.[7] The STPCD is the accumulation of years of experience and reflection by employment law experts; leaving head teachers and governing bodies to construct individual pay policies has seen too many of them embroiled in appeals against their pay progression decisions throughout November and December.

Head teachers can reject the worst elements of performance-related pay. We have to live by our values; the trouble is, head teachers are a mixed-ability group. I was at an association meeting not so long ago where a head teacher shrieked with barely controlled joy when she realised she did not have to match new recruits' existing pay grades 'because she wanted to save a bit of money'. On many levels it was a depressing moment.

---

[5] Michael Fullan and Andy Hargreaves, *Professional Capital: Transforming Teaching in Every School* (New York: Routledge, 2012).

[6] Michael Fullan, *The Six Secrets of Change: What the Best Leaders Do to Help Their Organizations Survive and Thrive* (San Francisco, CA: Jossey-Bass, 2011).

[7] Department for Education, School Teachers' Pay and Conditions Document 2014 and Guidance On School Teachers' Pay and Conditions (September 2014). Ref: DFE-00537-2014. Available at: https://www.gov.uk/government/publications/school-teachers-pay-and-conditions-2014.

As Daniel Pink says, 'Treat people like people.'[8] This principle is never more important than when it comes to paying teachers. In the end, performance-related pay generates fear in an institution, diverting colleagues from focusing entirely upon growing into truly great teachers. Performance-related pay is a corrosive policy which does nothing to improve the quality of teaching; I feel it is a nonsense in our school system.

This much I know about why it's not about the money

● Teachers are a school's most important resource and need to be treated accordingly.

● The vast majority of teachers are motivated by moral purpose and a selflessness to help others succeed, not by financial reward.

● Non-pecuniary benefits, such as high quality CPD provision, will be as attractive to teachers as any potential salary rise; remember, after tax, a basic Teaching and Learning Responsibility (TLR) payment equates to an extra Chinese takeaway a week.

● When it comes to assessing the quality of teaching, triangulate your evidence and use your wisdom when making a judgement.

● Design thorough, intelligent appraisal processes which reassure the governing body that teachers' performance is managed in a way which focuses upon continual improvement rather than summative judgement.

---

8 Daniel Pink, RSA Animate – Drive: The Surprising Truth About What Motivates Us [video] (1 April 2010). Available at: http://www.youtube.com/watch?v=u6XAPnuFjJc.

Chapter 15

Experience

The wheel of fortune

The years teach much which the days never know.

Ralph Waldo Emerson

In the early 1970s mother began cleaning for Mrs Mann whose house stood directly opposite the Piltdown golf course clubhouse. Mrs Mann was proper gentry; she was amongst the last to leave Norway in 1939 with the British ambassador. Her late husband had been influential at the golf club and the club championship was named after him – the Mann Salver.

Mrs Mann's house had a garden which backed on to the golf course and it wasn't long before she was employing dad as a gardener. It worked really well. Mother would clean every Friday and dad would garden after lunch on Tuesdays and Thursdays. The relationship between employer and employees grew strong.

There came a point in 1977 when Mrs Mann decided to move into the closest town, Uckfield. A small two-bedroomed cottage was attached to the converted barn she had bought and she offered the cottage to my dad. To leave the security of our council house was a big decision. And the cottage was smaller than it looked from outside, a sort of inverse Tardis, with one fewer bedrooms than we had at School Hill. It would mean mother and dad sleeping on a pull-out bed in the front room on a permanent basis.

Whilst there were downsides to moving, there were benefits too. The rent was cheaper, the post office was a minute's walk away and, again, my school was at the end of the road. So, in 1977 mother and dad took the biggest leap of faith in their lives and moved into Cherry Barn Cottage. And they never looked back.

Some of the financial pressures they had felt for decades suddenly lifted. Mrs Mann was generous and mother and dad were great for her; she had no family whatsoever, bar a very distant nephew. Mother kept her company daily whilst the garden was a rose-filled delight for dad. He was able to borrow her car, and with her family interest in golf Mrs Mann was keen to help fund my golf career. It worked for everyone.

They were modest, happy times. There were difficulties, but nothing that any family doesn't suffer at some point or another. By 1983 Mrs Mann had made it clear to mother and dad that she intended to leave all her worldly possessions to them: both houses, all her stocks and shares. The car. Everything. It was fortune beyond anything either had ever imagined. It was genuinely life changing.

Suddenly, dad could see the end of getting up at 4.15 a.m. every day except Sundays to go to the sorting office. He was 55 and would retire at 60, or earlier if circumstances allowed. It was a long way from the nights mother worked at Buxted Chicken factory in the 1960s, cutting off the legs of chickens with a pair of shears and coming home at 7 a.m. with blood blisters on her hands the size of two pence pieces. And she wouldn't have to 'do' for anyone else ever again.

When I teach *Of Mice and Men*, I always begin with the verse from Robbie Burns' poem, 'To a Mouse', from whence the title of Steinbeck's novel derives:

> But Mousie, thou art no thy lane,
> In proving foresight may be vain:
> The best-laid schemes o' mice an' men
> Gang aft agley,
> An' lea'e us nought but grief an' pain,
> For promis'd joy!

Dad had two years imagining his 'promis'd joy'. He died on 6 February 1985, six months before Mrs Mann passed away. Mother was left with all of Burns' 'grief an' pain' and a fortune she had no idea what to do with. She once said to me that she'd have been happy living in a hole in the ground with dad, rather than existing in the converted barn without him.

The whole experience left me a defensive pessimist. I am always hugely optimistic, in that I think we can achieve almost anything we want to, but I always plan anticipating that the worst will happen. My wife, on the other hand, would call me a doom-monger. But Oliver Burkeman, author of one of my favourite books, *The Antidote*, understands exactly why I operate as I do: 'Confronting the worst-case scenario saps it of much of its anxiety-inducing power. Happiness reached via positive thinking can be fleeting and brittle, negative visualisation generates a vastly more dependable calm.'[1]

And whilst what happened to us in the spring of 1985, as the wheel of fortune turned onwards and downwards, was truly dreadful, the wisdom I took from the experience was life enhancing.

Experience matters

We ignore the skills and resources that exist in older people at our peril.

Julia Unwin, chief executive of the Joseph Rowntree Trust

Old school and proud of it; that's how I describe Dave Lamb, our longest serving teacher. He's been at Huntington for thirty-five years since he began his teaching career in 1980. He is also head of house. He teaches resistant materials in a school where nearly every student follows a technology GCSE, the legacy of our now obsolete technology college status. In terms of examination results at Key Stage 4, the technology department is our most successful, bar none, and has been for getting on for two decades.

I met with Dave to see if I could surface what it is that is special about his pedagogy. There is more wisdom here than one might imagine; I feel sure that the lessons learnt from what Dave had to say could be the raw material for a whole new book.

---

[1] Oliver Burkeman, *The Antidote: Happiness for People Who Can't Stand Positive Thinking* (Edinburgh: Canongate Books, 2013).

With Dave's permission I publish extracts from our conversation, with students' names anonymised.

In conversation with Dave, 17 July 2013

John: I'm going to ask you a set of questions – is that OK?

Dave: Yes fine. It's difficult to talk about me without talking about the department.

John: It's about the cultural standards in your department, isn't it?

Dave: I have always been really lucky from the start – I have always worked in great departments. There are no egos; everybody helps each other. If anyone does a worksheet or anything for Key Stage 4 we will all share it. We team-teach and share expertise. No one is afraid to admit they need help – it works really well.

John: You have been here thirty-three years?

Dave: Yes. Dave X and Dave Y were metalwork teachers and I was a woodwork teacher and there were other woodwork teachers – and Tony who was an expert at everything – we were jacks-of-all-trades really. It was all much more skills based. It was different then – everyone grafted; it was about good relationships in the department. It was not as hard as it is now. We sit and have our lunch together, even if it is only ten minutes, we sit and chew the fat. We work hard and have a bit of a laugh, which is part and parcel of the whole thing. We have lots of very high expectations. When Steve came [as subject leader] he brought with him all the CAD/CAM – things that we cascade down. This works really well. He has also brought a real rigour. The way we address our Key Stage 4 kids now is very thorough. A good example of that is when we start the controlled assessments we tell them that we don't accept sloppy work. We are aware of targets and things but I will not let them start on any practical work that will get them less than a grade A [resistant materials at Huntington attracts students from across the whole attainment spectrum]. They may only be capable of getting a grade C, but there must be enough in that project that they are able to access those grades. We try to create an atmosphere that kids will buy into, and 95% of them will buy into what we are doing. We have some tricky kids over there, but Ben and Will bought into it for the most part.

John: How do you characterise that culture that they buy into?

Dave: We have a lot of fun with the kids. We set boundaries with them that they know they can't cross, but we do have a laugh. Steve and I team-teach for two hours on a Tuesday morning and there is a lot of banter with the kids and they love it. If you look at the work that Ben and Will produced practically – they worked and they kept their heads down. Because you can treat them a little bit differently – it is something they will engage with and get on with. We may not get a great set of exam results this year but everyone should get C or above and that is with the grade boundaries being raised every year. The work they have produced this year is of a higher standard. In the department we have a very hard-working culture. On Tuesdays, for instance, I will be in at 7 a.m. prepping the materials. We used to stay night after night getting technology finished. We don't let kids get behind – we are rigorous. Most of our projects were finished early this year – this is because we put in really early interventions. We are rigorous with the way we do things. Steve is great – he will go round and chase up kids if necessary – he is very supportive. That is what Steve has brought to the department. There is a lot of experience in the department; there are also kids in the department that you don't push too hard or they would walk away. You have to try to hit a level that works for them, that gets the most out of them, without making them thinking they are working too hard. As a department we just work bloody hard – no one falls out or anything. I am not saying it is utopia all the time, but we get on great.

John: Let me ask you a bit more about your teaching. How would you describe your teaching?

Dave: I try to make my teaching good as often as I can. Outstanding is a difficult ask these days, but my aim is to make my lessons good. Kids come into the class and say, 'Hi, Sir', and they go out and say, 'See you, Sir', and they have worked hard in the lesson.

John: In terms of your teaching, how do you plan your lessons?

Dave: It depends on the type of lesson. If it is Key Stage 4 I am a meticulous list writer – the night before I will plan so I know in my head which direction the work is going in. At Key Stage 4 we know the syllabus inside out. Sometimes it might seem boring, but we know what is going to get them good grades. Actually if you look at some of the [exam board] exemplar materials where they get a grade A, some of it is rubbish. We are working at a higher level of expectation, such as how well they make a door or how well they make a drawer. We get to manage CAD/CAM and how well they get all that together.

John: Your Key Stage 3 syllabus clearly prepares them well for Key Stage 4.

Dave: Yes, it does but we do a lot of joint-cutting practice, which is really old fashioned, but it's great. We give them lots of praise. I say to them that, with the mistakes they are making at the moment, they will not believe the standard they will be able to achieve by this time next year. We show them the exemplar work which we have got all over the place, which is really impor-tant. Kids like James, who was a bit of a silly boy, his drawing has come on in leaps and bounds. It's just simple and basic. I can't say I get it right all the time.

John: Your results suggest you get it right 99% of the time.

Dave: The results are based on us working bloody hard and making sure that the kids do not go down the wrong pathways.

It was funny when Steve first started – they tried to make one cabinet in the shape of a whale ... they didn't go down that route again! I am quite controlling. Some people might say that I am restricting the flair that they might show, but I want them to produce something that they will really enjoy and be proud of doing.

John: They can show that flair at Key Stage 4, can't they, in the quality of finish? It is just the tiny bits about finishing things off to get a grade A.

Dave: That's right. Kids like Tom this year, a statemented student, he has worked like stink. Every lesson he comes in and it is bang, bang, bang. We have had some difficult kids who have done really well. It is about creating a different atmosphere. It's time for these kids that is important – most of them will buy into it.

John: In terms of consciousness, what do you do in the way of feedback? How do you give feedback to the kids?

Dave: At Key Stage 4 you are giving individual feedback at every single lesson. You are having detailed conversations with them all the time which involves, 'What have you done wrong here? What is your next step?' – that sort of thing. It is constant feedback – every single kid, every lesson. Part and parcel of that is saying, 'This is a really tricky bit; you may be best coming after school to get it clamped up' and so on. And that is all of us. At Key Stage 3, 80–90% of the time it is practical work, so it's verbal feedback.

John: What about conscious stuff you do about literacy?

Dave: I consciously do a lot more about literacy than I ever used to. There used to be an unwritten rule that you changed the spelling of technical words and so on, but now we do a lot more than that. What we don't have in technology is extended pieces of writing, just short answers, so it is not a difficult thing to mark. I certainly do much more than I have ever done before.

John: What about prepping them for those exams?

Dave: At Key Stage 4 you get the theme. Ideally we would start prepping them a little bit earlier than we have managed before. We get the theme in March and that works well for resistant materials. The theme this year, for instance, was small portable storage and art deco, so you get the kids to start researching on the internet what art deco is and what its main features are. Some of the examinations are so predictable that you can almost guess what will come up. You can actually get them off to a good start on the paper so, for example, we spent a lot of time going through art deco features and we helped them to decide what small portable storage is. We looked at previous papers and at how those questions were formalised. We get them to practise doing timed sketches, so they know how long it takes to do them. By the time they have been through all of that they have enough to be able to adjust to whatever the question throws at them. Obviously without that practice with exam technique they could get behind on time. It is bang, crash, wallop – rigorous practice. Also if you put them under exam conditions they are more likely to work than if you were to send them away to research how to draw a design. Last year we had the best examination results for written examinations. I think this was down to thorough preparation and also because we kept them in school for so long.

John: What do you do to differentiate between students with different starting points?

Dave: At Key Stage 4 – I know this sounds like an old cliché but it's true – the work is self-differentiating. You have two aspects to the work: a design folder and the practical work. Some kids are very good practically but not traditionally academic – you have to know what the kids can actually do. They all have targets but you just have to see what they can do. Some of Steve's kids' design work in graphics this year is unbelievable. I am trying to aspire to that level this year. I think the design work

I have done with my Year 10 group is the best design work I have done so far. This is what Steve has brought – we help each other. I am happy with what I have produced so far. At Key Stage 3 the work is differentiated by their outcomes. In their folders, it is not like you are marking a massive piece of work – it is more short answers which are small pieces of information that they are responding to. In the past we had special folders with special language for SEND kids, but we found it wasn't really necessary. It is by nature an intimate subject – you have to have conversations with them and you work out what they are capable of and get them to keep moving on.

John: What advice would you give to new teachers in the profession?

Dave: I think teaching is a really hard job now. It is over-scrutinised and, in terms of the expectations and all the observations, it is really hard. The contact and the relationships with the kids is always the best thing. When I first started teaching I am not sure that I loved the kids at that time, but now I love the day-to-day interaction with them. That is the best part of it. I see the amount of endless plans that my wife has to produce to teach at primary school and nobody ever looks at them. She should be spending that time producing fantastic lessons. My advice to young teachers would be: make sure you know what you are doing and that you enjoy the job. It is not like other jobs; you have to go that extra mile. And that is what is good about our department – everybody goes the extra mile. Your day doesn't finish here; you are constantly doing the job. It is important that you know what you are getting into.

John: You can't do it half-heartedly, can you?

Dave: You certainly can't do it half-heartedly – it is not like that. That aspect has never changed.

John: Thanks – that was brilliant.

Dave: I don't feel I have said much …

We mustn't be seduced by the cult of youth or blinded by the dogmatism of experience. Like most successful things, schools need a blend of youth and experience and then the structures to enable both to learn from each other.

This much I know about experience

- The best schools are driven by wisdom and that is a rare commodity – make sure your wisest colleagues have a way of influencing policy and when they speak, listen.

- In a thirty-year career it is likely that you will be radical three times.

- Appoint the best teachers, even if that means they're the most expensive.

- Take a measured chance with youth; if they are ready, they're ready, no matter their age.

- Teaching is a young person's game generally – we have 112 teachers and, at the age of 50, only four of them are older than me.

Chapter 16

Making the time

Gone

How did it get so late so soon?

Dr Seuss

I have been forever obsessed with time. When I was taking my A levels I had a novel approach to making the absolute most of my time at the weekend. On Friday nights I would go to bed as late as possible. On Saturday mornings I would get up as early as I could. On Saturday nights I repeated my Friday night trick and my approach to Sunday mornings mirrored the one to Saturdays. I went to bed as late as I could on Sunday night. Exhausted, I spent the following week at school recovering.

The passage of time makes everything more precious. Daffodils, for instance, are important to me, chiefly because they are here with us fleetingly; they symbolise for me both the beginning of spring and the beautiful impermanence of things. And I love how we always remark upon the days getting longer in the springtime, even though it's an annual inevitability.

As Thomas Hardy might have said, my dad was one 'who noticed such things'.[1] Although he spent a lot of his life in the open air – on the golf course or delivering letters or gardening – my dad had the heart disease angina. He first had an attack aged 39. He was pushing my eldest brother, Dave, to run up to the rec to play football when he was seized by a sharp pain across his chest. He gripped, of all things, the metal gates to the village cemetery, waited for the pain to subside, turned around and walked Dave slowly home.

---

[1] Thomas Hardy, 'Afterwards', in *The Complete Poems*, ed. James Gibson (London: Palgrave Macmillan, 2001).

Over the years, dad's angina was an ever-present, unspoken worry for us all. When he felt a tightness in his chest he would pop a small white pill under his tongue and go to bed for the day. When we moved house he was particularly bad and, as a 12-year-old, it felt like our new life was going to be irreparably marred before it had begun. Due to his heart condition, he finally followed his doctor's advice and gave up smoking in 1980. Ironic, then, that five years later he died of cancer.

In the summer of 1984 I managed to secure a place at the University of York to study English. In late November I was sitting in one of Sid Bradley's Anglo-Saxon slide-show lectures when the college porter interrupted him and asked for me. There was a telephone call from home. I knew that dad had been poorly and was having his gall stones removed, but the news was much worse.

I came home to Sussex and found dad propped up in bed. The surgeon had made an incision, taken a quick look and sewed him back up again. There was nothing they could do. He was full of cancerous tumours. Dad couldn't remember much about what was said, but he knew he had about six weeks to live. He lasted ten.

It's hard to recall exactly what happened that Christmas. Dad said he just wanted a few quiet weeks. He didn't rage against the dying of the light; true to his character, he calmly accepted the inevitable. We bought him Christmas presents we knew he would never need. In marginal denial, my gift to him was a luxuriously thick woollen jumper, as though the warmth it would provide him would prove curative.

We had no religion. We assumed dad would go straight to heaven, whatever that meant. A Methodist preacher popped in having heard our sad news. Mother explained our simplistic thinking about dad's destiny; however, the preacher was unequivocal in his judgement that dad would not go to heaven as he hadn't taken Christ into his heart. Mother was devastated; she was sectioned and spent four of the last ten weeks dad was alive in hospital.

Dad's health declined rapidly. Once he dropped his fruit salad on the floor and proceeded to eat it off the carpet. We decided that I should return to York. He was deeply proud I'd made it to university and he didn't want his illness to affect my education.

I went back to university in the January. I don't know why I did that now. I've done some pretty stupid things in my fifty years but that is one of the very few I truly regret. Soon after I departed, dad jumped out of the bedroom window following a heroin-induced hallucination. He was admitted to the local hospital never to return home. He lasted another three weeks.

My dad was a modern stoic. We were obedient passives, in awe of medical opinion. When I asked mother why dad went into hospital she said, 'Your father was very poorly. It was taken out of our hands. The doctor made the decision.' She wasn't angry about it; it seems there was no choice. We accepted the professionals' decisions without challenge.

All my family was there the night before dad passed away except me. As he moved in and out of consciousness, family myth has it that he recognised my eldest brother and gave him one of his affectionate looks which said, 'You silly young fool!' They left him asleep at 9 p.m. Early the next morning, on 6 February 1985, just after 1 a.m., he died in a bed that was not his own, alone, aged just 57 years. I was in York, 250 miles away.

I was 20 years old when dad died and, until the age of 32 when we had our first son, Joe, the worst thing had already happened to me. As Hamlet said, 'there is nothing either good or bad, but thinking makes it so'. Dad's death only heightened my obsession with making the most of things whilst I have the time. There seems no point doing things which you don't want or don't need to do.

I have to admit that writing this book has been somewhat therapeutic; it preserves for me most of what I can still retrieve of my dad from my memory store. The only poem I've written about him of any worth, that was neither bitter nor mawkish, won the 1988 Robin Lee Memorial Poetry Prize at the University of Sussex.

Memorial

I

The dark of an
Anglo-Saxon
slide show – scrambling
to complete a

Milton essay
in the lecture
hall's dimmed corner.
Undercover

operations
exposed by the
porter's message –
Urgent: 'phone home.

I didn't know,
(but really knew)
what was afoot.
Father's minor

operation –
just routine, but
mother's voice broke
cancerous news.

II

The fast train slows
softly into
London's King's Cross,
echoing its

entry into
York. Between the
two the journey
was smooth – contin-

uation 'til
destination
assured. The last
few miles are the

worst – knowing the
end is near but
not knowing when.
Suddenly it's

over, ended
before it began.
Terminated.

III
Energetic
Jack Russells find
solemnity
impossible.

This canine shows
death scant respect,
resists my self-
imposed sorrow,

pulls me away
from the marble
memorial,
out the graveyard

gate, barking and
panting, alive
with riotous
celebration.

Structuring our time to get better

> You will never 'find' time for anything. If you want time, you must make it.
>
> Charles Buxton

If school leaders have one priority, it is to create in their schools the conditions for growth for their students and staff. As school budgets tighten across the globe in this age of austerity, you have to resist the urge to squeeze every last hour of teaching out of your teachers; rather, you must give your teachers time and space to work on their practice.

There is no short cut to being a great teacher. I reckon Dylan Wiliam got it right when he said, 'Elite performance is the result of at least a decade of maximal efforts to improve performance through an optimal distribution of deliberate practice.'[2] Trouble is, you can't just insist that colleagues work on their teaching. Yoon and colleagues have provided evidence suggesting that CPD lasting less than thirty hours has never been found to affect student outcomes.[3]

Tom Bentley's mantra, which I heard him say years ago at a National College of School Leadership conference, is unbeatable when it comes to ensuring you have coherent focus in your school: 'Change your structures to accommodate your core purpose, rather than contort your core purpose to fit within your existing structures.' It has underpinned my approach to school leadership ever since.

Like an increasing number of schools, we have two hours of CPD time every fortnight as well as our five standard training days – that's a minimum of sixty-three hours of CPD a year. In the nineteen two-hour

---

[2] Wiliam, How Do We Prepare Our Students for a World We Cannot Possibly Imagine?

[3] Kwang Suk Yoon, Theresa Duncan, Silvia Wen-Yu Lee, Beth Scarloss and Kathy L. Shapley, *Reviewing the Evidence On How Teacher Professional Development Affects Student Achievement.* Issues & Answers Report, REL 2007-No. 033 (Washington, DC: US Department of Education, Institute of Education Sciences, National Center for Education Evaluation and Regional Assistance, Regional Educational Laboratory Southwest).

sessions a year, departments can focus on their development priorities and teachers can co-plan lessons and work on their teaching.

We have less than the government's recommended contact time with students, but since we introduced the restructured school time-table our results have improved significantly. It is far better for students to get less contact time but for that contact time with teachers to be of a high quality, rather than more time exposed to mediocre teaching. À la Bentley, we have changed our structure to accommodate our core purpose.

Our annual nineteen two-hour sessions, every fortnight, are known as our Teaching and Learning Forum (TLF). The TLF sessions are based in subject areas, with seven of them beginning with an hour together as a whole staff watching and debating examples of our practice on video. The TLFs give colleagues time to talk about which aspects of their teaching they are currently developing. It's about improving practice at the micro-level – gesture, questioning, subtle classroom control techniques, as well as focusing upon improving subject knowledge – and sharing with colleagues the trials and tribulations of trying to get better at this thing called 'teaching'.

This golden thread from teaching through to student outcomes underpins our approach to improving teaching, and echoes Professor Rob Coe's assertion that great teaching is defined as 'that which leads to improved student progress.'[4]

Each teacher's personal development is charted by the individual teacher in her Growing Great Teachers Professional Development Journal where she keeps a record of exactly how she is working on her teaching as part of her professional obligation to improve her practice. What we are doing is ensuring that we all have the space and time to work deliberately and continuously upon our practice and, having dispensed with attending expensive external courses which promise to move you to outstanding, we have confidence within ourselves to support each other to improve our teaching. To create such a culture,

---

[4] Coe et al., *What Makes Great Teaching?*

ring-fenced, frequent, regular periods of time dedicated to improving teaching are an utterly essential ingredient of the self-improving school.

A checklist to help you decide whether your school organisation is conducive to growing great teachers is provided with some spirit by Saphier, King and D'Auria:

> Are teachers spending time on items related to academic focus? Does their talk reflect real belief in the students and shared responsibility? Can they engage one another in honest, non-defensive dialogue? If the answer is yes, then 'Katie, bar the door!' This school is going somewhere![5]

We have to create the structures for our teaching teams to work together. How often do we hear our colleagues say, 'We have no time'? Our greatest resource is our teachers and their most precious resource is their time; it is common sense, then, that we must give our greatest resource the time to learn to become even better teachers.

This much I know about making the time

- You have to privilege the time for teachers to work on their teaching if you want to grow a truly great school.

- Beware of asking colleagues to do anything which impinges on their time without it being to their benefit.

- Work in twenty-five-minute chunks and use the Pomodoro Technique[6] – I swear by it!

- Cut corners if you have to – sometimes *just* good enough *is* good enough.

- Some things just won't get done. Period.

---

[5] Jon Saphier, Matt King and John D'Auria, 3 Strands Form Strong School Leadership, *National Staff Development Council* 27(2) (2006): 51–57.

[6] See http://pomodorotechnique.com/.

Chapter 17

Becoming an evidence-based profession

Relationships, relationships, relationships …

Think where man's glory most begins and ends
And say my glory was I had such friends.

W. B. Yeats, 'The Municipal Gallery Revisited'

Any head teacher knows how important it is to have great support staff, and John Cobb, one of our excellent caretaking team, is up there with the best. When we interviewed him he was concerned that the work pattern would interfere with his passion – pigeon racing.

Since I appointed John we have spent many moments sharing our knowledge of the countryside, one of which occurred as I was leaving work one summer evening. He told me about how, when he had crossed the mist-shrouded River Ouse early that morning, he was reminded of his dawn-start fishing trips with his dad fifty years before. His reminiscences were a sonnet waiting to be written.

Fishing Lines

for John

His old man crossed the landing to his room
And, careful not to wake the eldest son,
He whispered to the youngest through the gloom
The needless exhortation, *John, come on.*
The weather's good. And like two guilty thieves
They rode unnoticed through the early dawn;
A getaway on bikes along York's streets
To *Puncture Bridge.* The morning mist adorned
The slow, resplendent Ouse – just like this June,
Fifty years on. Those stolen early starts,

Sat with his dad beneath the fading moon,
Were when he learnt the expert angler's art:
When to *strike*, how to read the river's flow –
Such things that only fishermen can know.

There is no quantitative evidence to say that relationships matter more than anything else in life; it's just something I was taught by my dad and something I have come to know over the years.

I have grown to appreciate that there is always a proverbial silver lining. Dad's angina meant he was given his own post van and a single round through the country lanes south of Uckfield. It took the pressure off him walking and having to carry a heavy bag of post. What it afforded him was the chance to forge strong, life-enriching relationships with the men and women to whom he delivered letters.

One of his friendships from which I benefitted directly was with Norman and Guy, the two housekeepers at Arches Manor. Hugh Vaughan-Thomas, Glamorgan cricketer and brother of the BBC radio presenter Wynford, owned Arches but was rarely there.

Norman and Guy loved my dad and allowed me to fish the manor's carp pool whilst the three of them drank wine and danced to Dolly Parton singing 'Stand By Your Man'. I was a bit rubbish at the fishing, thinking that the bigger the fish – and there were some monster carp in that ancient pond – the more bait you had to use; the footballs of bread I cast out as bait must have been completely uneatable. But the summer evenings, sat stock still with the hair frozen on my head for what I might catch, were awesome in the true sense of the word.

Dad's round incorporated Framfield where my sister Heather now lives. Before she moved into her house it was owned by an old man and dad used to deliver his letters. After the old man died and his daughter had sold Heather the house, she took my sister by the hand and led her out to the back garden.

There, at the far end of the lawn, a hole had been dug in the ground, remarkably similar in size to a golf hole. Apparently dad would stop at the old man's house, on occasion, for a cup of tea and had taught him how to putt.

The home-made hole in the lawn was just one of the many legacies dad left the people he greeted daily with their letters. When he died mother did not feel able to give dad's Jack Russell dog, Jilly, the daily walks she needed. We gave Jilly to a couple who ran a farm on dad's round. I saw Jilly once after that, in the town in the back of a car, and she went as wild at seeing me as she had done with dad in his car, years before, on the way to the golf course to chase rabbits.

I was closest to my dad for two days in the summer of 1978 when I was just 13. I played in the South East qualifying round of the *Daily Express* Junior Golf Championship at Liphook Golf Club in Hampshire. Dad took two days off work, borrowed Mrs Mann's white Mini and we stayed with my godmother, Auntie Joan, in her high-rise flat in Havant.

Cars are great places to talk about profound things. If you have a teenage son who needs to tell you something, pop him in the passenger seat and drive – he'll open up in minutes because he can converse with you whilst you both stare straight ahead. So we travelled to Liphook via Havant, just me and dad, chatting. Auntie Joan's full English breakfast that cool warm morning was spectacular.

When we arrived at the course the day was clear with pure sunshine. Dad wished me good luck and then vanished. I began shakily with a poor tee shot on the par three first hole but then went on to score 74 and finish third. My crisis point in the round came at the seventeenth hole where I fluffed a chip shot. I could have panicked and ruined things. Instead I walked away, composed myself and proceeded to hole a 30 foot putt from off the green to save my par.

When I had finished in front of the Liphook clubhouse, dad suddenly appeared again. After the prize-giving, we drove home and talked through my round. He'd watched near every shot and I'd had no idea. He'd stolen round the course amongst the undergrowth, tracking my progress. He'd shared in my greatest round of golf to date without me knowing. He was particularly praiseworthy of how I'd handled the crisis at the seventeenth. If I have the ability to remain calm, it comes from my dad.

Only when you're a dad yourself do you understand better your own. He must have been so proud of my golfing achievements, but he never let his pride affect his wisdom. When I was offered a job at 16 as an assistant professional at a golf course in Holyhead, he stopped me accepting the chance to be paid next to nothing as a shop assistant, living alone in a caravan on the very edge of the we(tte)st coast of the country; I have a lot to thank dad for, but I genuinely cannot thank him enough for saving me from that dank fate. I only hope I can provide such wisdom for my boys, Joe and Oliver, when they need it.

Dad was beloved by many and all; the week after he died even the main Piltdown Golf Club flew their club flag at half-mast. He taught me and my siblings that relationships matter above everything else, that kindness always wins out in the end and that you should treat people as you find them, without prejudice and without exception.

How can we become an evidence-based profession?

Tom Bennett @tombennett71 · May 3
Apparently @johntomsett just said 'People are what matters'. WHERE'S HIS EVIDENCE oh God I'm having a breakdown #ntenred

Maybe the title of this chapter should be 'Do we need to become an evidence-based profession?' There's a spectrum of opinion when it comes to evidence-based approaches to educational policy-making. At one end you have Gert Biesta who says, 'an exclusive emphasis upon "what works" will simply not work,'[1] and at the other end we have Tim Harford who believes that, 'When considering an intervention which might profoundly affect people's lives, there is one thing more unethical than running a randomised controlled trial, it's not running the trial.'[2] I'll return to the spectrum later, but for now I want us to think about Masie Tubbs.

---

[1] Gert J. J. Biesta, Why 'What Works' Won't Work: Evidence-Based Practice and the Democratic Deficit of Educational Research, *Educational Theory* 57(1) (2007): 1–22.

[2] Tim Harford, The Random Risks of Randomised Controlled Trials, *Tim Harford* (1 May 2014). Available at: http://timharford.com/2014/04/the-random-risks-of-randomised-trials/.

Masie Tubbs is a 36-year-old woman. She attained a first-class honours degree and went straight into teaching after her PGCE. She teaches full time and has two children. Her students make good progress and their examination results at GCSE and A level are good, year in, year out. She teaches good lessons, and students and parents speak highly of her. She meets all her administrative deadlines. She leaves school at 4 p.m. every day, but does two or three hours of work most nights when the children are in bed. Her husband works full time too and is away overnight once or twice a week. Why on earth does she need to read any educational research?

Yet Dylan Wiliam reckons 'every teacher needs to improve ... because they can be even better'.[3] So how can we engage Masie Tubbs in research which will help her to improve her practice at the margins? Masie will probably read a half-side of A4 summary of some research findings on effective feedback. But, as Wiliam points out, even if Masie reads the research digest and changes her mind about feedback, it probably won't have any impact upon her practice: 'The last 30 years have shown conclusively that you can change teachers' thinking about something without changing what those teachers do in classrooms.'[4] The frustrating thing is, the vast amount of high quality research into pedagogy means we know what works. The trouble is, too few teachers read the research; even fewer act upon it.

I agree entirely with Professor Rob Coe when he says, 'it is time we established a more scientific approach [to school improvement]'.[5] We have to stop guessing about what works. School budgets are getting tighter and tighter; it is even more important, then, that every penny we have left to spend impacts positively upon improving the quality of teaching and through to student outcomes.

---

[3] Dylan Wiliam, How Do We Prepare Our Students for a World We Cannot Possibly Imagine?

[4] Dylan Wiliam, Changing Classroom Practice, *Educational Leadership* 65(4) (2007/8): 36–42.

[5] Coe, Improving Education.

Dr Jonathan Sharples, who is currently working with the Education Endowment Foundation (EEF),[6] encapsulates as strong an argument as any for developing an evidence-based teaching profession in his *Evidence for the Frontline*. It is hard to disagree with him when he writes, 'Inevitably, too many important decisions are made by best guesses and are overly influenced by politics, marketing, anecdotal evidence and tradition. This results in classic pendulum swings, where new ideas and practices are enthusiastically embraced, found wanting and abandoned, only to be rediscovered in cycles.'[7] Every single one of us now teaching in this country's schools has tried a school improvement strategy without questioning its effectiveness beforehand (has anyone, for instance, evaluated the impact of school house systems, which, post-*Harry Potter*, seem to be back in vogue?).

We need to ensure that our knowledge about what exactly helps children to learn impacts upon our classroom practice. We haven't got the money to experiment wildly to find out what works, and we don't need to; improving teaching is about working deliberately at the margins of our practice. At Huntington we use our educated intuition about what works, alongside the relevant educational research, to shape our school improvement strategies. We focus heavily upon the implementation of strategies and we evaluate, evaluate, evaluate. It is a model we are refining with the help of Dr Jonathan Sharples; we are intent upon becoming a (cost-efficient) research-centred school.

The Sutton Trust-EEF *Teaching and Learning Toolkit*, which summarises in one document meta-analyses of the main strategies used to improve student outcomes, is a huge step towards helping schools base their school improvement plans upon evidence.[8] The *Toolkit*

---

[6] See http://educationendowmentfoundation.org.uk/.

[7] Jonathan Sharples, *Evidence for the Frontline* (London: Alliance for Useful Evidence, 2013). Available at: http://www.alliance4usefulevidence.org/ publication/evidence-for-the-frontline/.

[8] Steve Higgins, Maria Katsipataki, Dimitra Kokotsaki, Robbie Coleman, Lee Elliot Major and Robert Coe, *The Sutton Trust–Education Endowment Foundation Teaching and Learning Toolkit* (London: Education Endowment Foundation, 2013).

was originally designed to help schools spend their pupil premium funding most effectively. No surprise, then, that head teachers suddenly leapt upon the *Toolkit* once the link with the pupil premium and then Ofsted was made. Head teachers were suddenly producing heavily annotated copies of the *Toolkit* to flash in front of the lead inspector on the first day of inspection.

What is troubling is that, in the same way that teachers can read research but not change what they do in the classroom, head teachers can read the *Toolkit* and not change the way they implement and then, crucially, evaluate their school improvement initiatives. It is potentially very useful, but will head teachers ever use it effectively to systematically inform the leadership of their schools? As John Dunford, the pupil premium champion, said: 'There is strong evidence out there about what works in closing the achievement gap – perhaps more evidence than in any other area education … however, one of the problems is that schools, like government ministers, often don't refer to research to influence policy and practice. Far too many changes are made without the best use of evidence, so one of my jobs will be to emphasise what works and to get those messages across.'[9]

The follow-up document to the *Teaching and Learning Toolkit* has been the *DIY Evaluation Guide*.[10] It's a foolproof, step-by-step guide to evaluating your own improvement initiatives. It's a great piece of work, but, I fear, the twelve-stage process from diagnosis to evaluation will be rarely used in schools.

We developed a case study of a matched trial based precisely upon the *DIY Evaluation Guide* to determine whether oral feedback, as well as written feedback, to a Year 9 class was more effective in improving

---

[9]   Quoted in Dorothy Lepkowska, Meet the National Pupil Premium Champion, *SecEd* (12 September 2013). Available at: http://www.sec-ed.co.uk/best-practice/meet-the-national-pupil-premium-champion.

[10]   Robert Coe, Stuart Kime, Camilla Nevill and Robbie Coleman, *The DIY Evaluation Guide* (London: Education Endowment Foundation, 2013) Available at: http://educationendowmentfoundation.org.uk/uploads/pdf/EEF_DIY_ Evaluation_Guide_(2013).pdf.

students' writing than merely written feedback. The outcome was a 0.34 effect size which confirmed our educated intuition that talking to individual students about how to improve their writing would be better than just letting them read our comments. As far as I know, this is one of very few case studies based upon the excellent *DIY Evaluation Guide*. In the same way that Masie Tubbs has no time to read the research, you have head teachers without the headspace to think about detailed implementation and evaluation of improvement strategies.

At researchED 2013, Kevan Collins, director of the EEF, introduced its 'applying evidence in practice' cycle:[11]

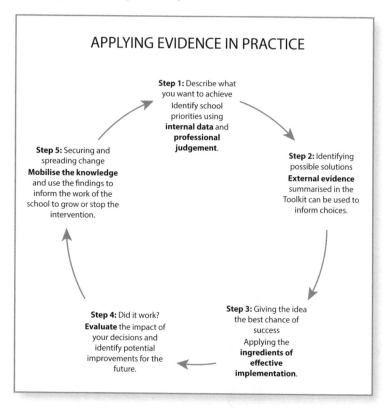

APPLYING EVIDENCE IN PRACTICE

Step 1: Describe what you want to achieve
Identify school priorities using **internal data** and **professional judgement**.

Step 2: Identifying possible solutions
External evidence summarised in the Toolkit can be used to inform choices.

Step 3: Giving the idea the best chance of success
Applying the **ingredients of effective implementation**.

Step 4: Did it work?
Evaluate the impact of your decisions and identify potential improvements for the future.

Step 5: Securing and spreading change
Mobilise the knowledge and use the findings to inform the work of the school to grow or stop the intervention.

---

[11] Kevan Collins, Putting the Evidence Into Action: Bridging the Gap Between Research and Practice [video] (27 September 2013). Available at: http://www.youtube.com/watch?v=YvzK7yJ2Euk.

It's genuine simplicity, but beneath each stage there is a great deal of thinking. For instance, under Step 4 ask yourself this question: 'In an evaluation of an intervention, what steps can you take to ensure that the intervention you intended to evaluate is actually what happens? What else could happen that might explain any differences (or lack of them) at the end of the treatment?' It isn't easy stuff. It isn't stuff that most head teachers have ever thought about that deeply. It's certainly not what you might learn about on the National Professional Qualification for Headship.

What attracts me to the EEF's applying evidence in practice cycle, however, is how it chimes almost perfectly with our own model of self-evaluation. For years we have tried hard to stick to a simple process of school improvement (outlined below):

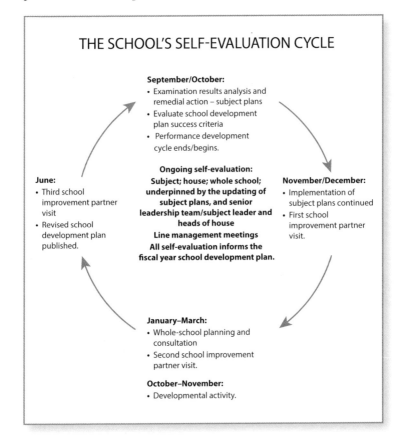

THE SCHOOL'S SELF-EVALUATION CYCLE

September/October:
- Examination results analysis and remedial action – subject plans
- Evaluate school development plan success criteria
- Performance development cycle ends/begins.

Ongoing self-evaluation:
Subject; house; whole school; underpinned by the updating of subject plans, and senior leadership team/subject leader and heads of house
Line management meetings
All self-evaluation informs the fiscal year school development plan.

November/December:
- Implementation of subject plans continued
- First school improvement partner visit.

January–March:
- Whole-school planning and consultation
- Second school improvement partner visit.

October–November:
- Developmental activity.

June:
- Third school improvement partner visit
- Revised school development plan published.

It includes one or two things the EEF don't have to think about, like funding and seventh/twelfth to fifth/twelfth fiscal years. We have always planned improvement based upon student outcomes and obsessively evaluated the impact of our improvement activities against our examination results down to the individual student level. The thing is, the quality of our evaluations is nowhere near as rigorous as I'd like it to be; as any head teacher will know, evaluating the impact of individual strategies is a complex business because the number of variables in a school of 1,500 students is immense.

Still, despite being pretty certain that we should become an evidence-based profession, there are a number of related questions which nag away at me: is research the new VAK? Is research just the next educational fad? Does research actually make any difference in schools? Will we see the big companies exploit this particular flavour of the month with a whole rash of expensive conferences about research?

We are now embarked upon running a Randomised Controlled Trial (RCT) with the EEF into the effectiveness of research on improving students' outcomes which will run over four years. It's an amazing learning experience as we are working on the project with the EEF, the Institute of Education and Professor Rob Coe from CEM at Durham. We want to see if the applying evidence in practice cycle really does refine school improvement processes and, by doing so, increase the impact of school improvement activities.

We think – or more precisely, we have an educated intuition – that having a director of research for teaching and learning at the heart of the school is the best model for helping research evidence to impact upon students' outcomes via the teachers' improved pedagogy. We will deliver a high quality training programme which will help senior leaders of our treatment schools to become much more efficient at implementing and evaluating school improvement initiatives. We will then evaluate whether that intervention has any impact whatsoever upon the outcomes of the students in those treatment schools compared to the outcomes of the students in the control schools.

One of the aspects of our RCT which makes me smile is that, as deliverers of the training programme, we cannot be involved in the real thing – we are too 'contaminated', a technical research term apparently. Hopefully, however, by October 2017, we will be able to tell the world whether or not research is the new Brain Gym.

The thing is, as Daniel Willingham has pointed out, 'knowing what to believe is a problem',[12] which is probably why research-centred schools are hard to find. King Edward VI Grammar School in Chelmsford seems to have systematically embedded research within the school's DNA; their Learning Lessons website is well worth a look.[13] And Linda Marshall has woven research into the weft and warp of Bradford Academy.[14] But these examples of research-centred schools are rare beasts.

To develop the researched-centred school so that we have a system-wide network will take some time. In 2012, American professor of psychology Daniel Willingham hoped that someone 'would see it as part of their mission to improve teachers' practice by providing authoritative information about the scientific reliability of various changes.'[15] Ben Goldacre developed the theme in the UK the following year with his paper, 'Building Evidence Into Education', co-launched at a conference in London with then Secretary of State for Education Michael Gove.[16]

---

[12] Daniel T. Willingham, *When Can You Trust the Experts? How To Tell Good Science from Bad in Education* (San Francisco, CA: Jossey-Bass, 2012).

[13] See http://www.kegs.org.uk/learning-lessons-archive--vol-1/265164.html.

[14] See Linda Marshall, Building a Research-Based Culture in a School: A Personal Perspective from a Headteacher, *Teaching Leaders Quarterly* Q2/13: 9–11. Available at: http://www.teachingleaders.org.uk/wp-content/uploads/2013/12/building-a-research-based-culture_Quarterly_Q2-13-4.pdf.

[15] Willingham, *When Can You Trust the Experts?*

[16] Ben Goldacre, Building Evidence Into Education (March 2013). Available at: http://media.education.gov.uk/assets/files/pdf/b/ben%20goldacre%20paper.pdf.

Soon afterwards Tom Bennett, author of *Teacher Proof*, took up the metaphorical research baton and with Hélène Galdin-O'Shea, promoted the researchED 2013 conference which saw a relatively small number of research-inspired teachers gather together to form what could develop into a foundation upon which to build a research-informed profession.[17]

Ben Goldacre, in his keynote speech at researchED 2013, talked about what can be achieved in 'a decade or two, a generation or three', about how teachers and researchers can network to find out what works and to do it.[18] He said that it will take time and 'spods'.[19] People like me are, according to Goldacre, spods, and if we are going to see evidence-based practice widespread in teaching we'll need a few more spods yet. Encouragingly, researchED continues to thrive under Tom Bennett's leadership.

Reflecting further upon this issue, I feel that if we are going to see evidence-based policy-making in schools then initial teacher training will need to change. I'm lamenting the orchestrated dismantling of the university PGCE. The ITT courses at the University of York, for instance, are extraordinarily good compared to my training on the PGCE English course at the University of Sussex in the late 1980s.

The PGCE at York has a research project as an integral element of the course. The course designers deliberately highlight the importance of being able to interpret and undertake educational research. Teachers as learners from the outset – it's the only way. Whatever is replacing the modern university-based PGCE must have a distinct research element

---

[17] See http://www.researched2013.co.uk/.

[18] Ben Goldacre, keynote speech at researchED 2013, London, 7 September 2013. Available at: http://www.researched2013.co.uk/ben-goldacres-keynote-at-researched-2013/.

[19] The website www.urbandictionary.com defines spod as: n. Chiefly British slang. One who spends an inordinate amount of time exchanging remarks in computer chatrooms or participating in discussions in newsgroups or on bulletin boards. Words related to spod include geek, nerd and boredom.

if we are going to have a research-informed profession in 'a decade or two, a generation or three'.

I also wonder whether, in fact, evidence-based policy-making will only ever become a reality in a school if its biggest advocate is the head teacher. I remember as a deputy head being told by my boss, Chris Bridge, that as a deputy you can only do something if the head teacher wants it to happen. In most schools the head teacher has an impressive power of veto.

As is my wont, I would claim that if we want to increase the influence of research and develop evidence-based policy-making then we need to change our structures. At the heart of our new director of teaching and learning's brief is developing research-informed practice, working vertically within Huntington and horizontally across collaborations regionally and nationally. And it's important to allocate a decent amount of leadership and management time to the role: you cannot expect people to do an expert job if they do not have the time in which to do that job expertly.

Understanding the validity and import of research findings is another thing altogether. Even if we read the research, how do we know if it can help us, or whether it's worth anything anyway? If we are interested in using research to inform our practice we need a short checklist of questions to ask about the research to allow us to know whether it's worth its constituent pixels. Alex Quigley demonstrated an excellent understanding of how to judge the authority of research findings in two posts on his blog, *HuntingEnglish*, where he concluded that, 'We should scrutinise the evidence for the "how", the "who" and the "why".'[20] Indeed, part of our EEF RCT intervention will be to mentor school-based research leads on how best to select research evidence to inform classroom practice.

---

[20] Alex Quigley, A Cautionary Tale of Educational Evidence – Part 2, *Hunting English* (14 February 2014). Available at: http://www.huntingenglish.com/2014/02/14/cautionary-tale-evidence-education-part-2/.

Having undertaken a small piece of research at Huntington into the effectiveness of oral feedback for Year 9 English students, I think the teacher as researcher model is incredibly flawed. It's pointless doing research which ticks the research box but which doesn't improve the impact of teaching upon students' learning. At researchED 2013 Ben Goldacre was clearly saddened by all those action research projects undertaken by highly committed teachers which are, to use his words, 'methodologically crap'. And yet … Ron Berger says this about his colleagues who have embarked on research into their own pedagogy:

> In the past 10 years I've had the privilege of spending time with many teachers who are investigating their practice. The excitement and knowledge that they develop is universal. Just like with students, the pressure that comes with making their work public compels them to put unusual effort and thoughtfulness into their practice.[21]

Is it possible to undertake a research project which has no discernable impact upon your students' performance but which makes you a more deliberate, reflective practitioner? I do think such a thing is possible but I'm not certain. As far as I am concerned, teacher research has to address questions to which teachers really need an answer.

Once you know what works, checklists are really helpful. If we have established that a certain practice has a positive impact on student outcomes, and if we all adopted it students would benefit significantly, then we create a simple way for teachers to check they have adopted it until it becomes hardwired into their brains. Checklists have certainly worked as part of our lesson maps, discussed earlier in Chapter 9 on lesson planning.

Another issue for the research world is scalability. If you have good evidence that something works, how do you get that knowledge into schools, into the hands of teachers and impacting upon learning? Some of the most influential research is influential because it is well-packaged. *Inside the Black Box* had a snappy title and it was a wonderfully

---

[21] Berger, *An Ethic of Excellence*.

thin, easily read pamphlet. Carol Dweck has repackaged her mindset work in a best-selling book, *Mindset: The New Psychology of Success.* Packaging your research evidence effectively is a crucial step in ensuring that it affects classroom pedagogy.

Finally, our raw materials are not wood and steel. As I've mentioned, we worked recently with Dr Jonathan Sharples on shaping a research project. What became clear from Jonathan is that it is almost impossible to isolate a single variable and eliminate all the other variables when conducting research in schools. Undertaking research in a way that is methodologically sound is challenging. Partnerships with professional researchers are critical if teachers are going to complete research which has any chance of being credible and, consequently, of any value for the teachers themselves.

Maybe we shouldn't worry too much about Masie Tubbs. Maybe it's young teachers like Jen Ludgate – in her third year of teaching, already assistant leader of the English faculty and co-director of #TLT2013 and #TLT2014 – who we should be inspiring to engage in a meaningful and sustained way with educational research. Inspire her now and she might be inspired to be research-savvy for a whole career; and she's more important than me as I have only ten career years left. Don't inspire her and, as Rivkin and colleagues established through their research, she's unlikely to consciously improve her practice significantly for the rest of her career: 'There appear to be important gains in teaching quality in the first year of experience and smaller gains over the next few career years. However, there is little evidence that improvements continue after the first three years.'[22] There's little time to lose.

Until we establish the Holy Grail of research-centred schools then, perhaps, all we can do is follow Professor Rob Coe's advice when he says, 'Our strategy should therefore be to make the best choices we can from the best evidence available, to try it out, with an open mind, and see if it works. If it does, we can keep doing it; if not, we will learn from that experience and try something else.'[23]

---

[22] Rivkin et al., Teachers, Schools, and Academic Achievement.

[23] Coe, Improving Education.

And at the moment, when it comes to that Biesta–Harford spectrum, I feel most closely aligned to the scientist Arthur Eddington, who remarked in 1935 that 'Observation and theory get on best when they are mixed together, both helping one another in the pursuit of truth.'[24] It would be contradictory folly to assume any other stance on the matter until we have concluded our EEF-sponsored RCT into the efficacy of research in schools. Ask me in October 2017 and I may well have changed my mind!

This much I know about becoming an evidence-based profession

Teaching will only become an evidence-based profession when a leadership wisdom prevails which creates structures in schools where classroom teachers:

- Work in an environment where continual improvement is the cultural norm.

- Can access good evidence easily.

- Feel encouraged and safe to change their practice in the light of the evidence.

- Are supported by a school-based research lead with a higher education connection.

- Can evaluate the impact on student outcomes of the changes to their pedagogy.

---

[24] Cited in the abstract of Stefano Lenci, Giuseppe Rega and Laura Ruzziconi, The Dynamical Integrity Concept for Interpreting/Predicting Experimental Behaviour: From Macro- to Nano-Mechanics, *Philosophical Transactions A* (2013). Available at: http://rsta.royalsocietypublishing.org/content/371/1993/20120423?cited-by=yes&legid=roypta;371/1993/20120423.

Chapter 18

Tending your colleagues

An Arthur Miller life lesson

> As I go around the world and ask those I meet what matters
> most to them, they all say their family comes first.
>
> Antony Jenkins, CEO of Barclays

I'm not sure everyone who says his or her family comes first really means it; I now know that I didn't. When I began blogging back in June 2012 I used the 'This Much I Know' format, plagiarised from the *Observer* magazine. That first blog post resonated with many readers and this final bullet point seemed to touch people most:

> **To some extent, I missed my eldest son growing up.** Joe is 15 years old now and a young man. When I cuddle him I can't believe the width of his shoulders and he squirms away as quick as he can. He thinks I'm an idiot! Read *Death of a Salesman* if you want to know why you should spend more time with the people you love. I taught it last year and now, whenever my sons ask me to do something, I do it, irrespective of my work.[1]

Between 1998, when I was appointed deputy head teacher at Huntington School in York, and a February day in 2011 when Miller's play awoke me, Joe morphed from a 2-year-old toddler into a young man; metaphorically I had slept through the whole process.

We always wanted our house to be an open house. We planned for it to ring with youthful laughter. We hoped it would be a second home to

---

[1] This Much I Know (With Apologies to the Observer Magazine), *John Tomsett* (16 June 2012). Available at: http://johntomsett.com/2012/06/16/ this-much-i-know-with-apologies-to-the-observer-magazine/.

all our sons' friends. We imagined it alive with bright, young faces. But I put my work first and our dream died.

I didn't mean to be a misery but I know I was. I would take Joe to football on a Sunday morning when he played for the under 9s knowing I had a technology college bid to write. I would be moody when the kick-off was delayed. I would be mad with him when he didn't try. I felt like he was wasting my time – time when I could have been working.

When his mates turned up, I would snap at them when they were rowdy, growl at them when they had a popcorn fight in the front room, bark at them to be quiet in the early days during the rare sleepovers at ours – because I had to get up early to work. They soon grew afeard and Joe went to their houses to watch the footie, to hang out and to lark around because their folks were much more fun.

Despite the obvious signs of failure to connect with Joe, I ploughed on with my career. I secured one headship then another. Headships are all-consuming things; you're a head teacher every minute of every day. And my designation became Joe's vehicle for abuse. 'Stop being a head teacher' he would mutter with no attempt to conceal his contempt for me.

I justified my work obsession through the middle-class lifestyle it afforded us as a family, even though I knew that was nonsense. I ended up working even longer hours; coming home late meant I didn't get to eat tea with my wife and the boys. In so many ways I was an absent father, though present every day. And the gulf between me and Joe grew wider.

So it was, teaching A level English on that day in February 2011, that Arthur Miller's insight changed my life. Near the end of *Death of a Salesman* Willy Loman clashes with his son, Biff; as they fight Biff suddenly kisses him. Willy is astounded. He says, '(after a long pause, astonished, elevated): Isn't that – isn't that remarkable? Biff – he likes me!'

We were watching the Dustin Hoffman film version of the play before we got to read the text. I'd never seen the play and so, with the students,

I was watching it for the first time. Biff's kiss and Willy's response destroyed me. I had to leave the room, weeping uncontrollably. The students were bemused whilst my colleague Jane provided me tissues in wordless confusion as I fled to an office across the corridor.

A myriad of different issues surfaced in that classroom: my own postman dad's sense of futility having spent forty-two years delivering letters and dying three years before he could retire to tend his roses; my sense of failure at being unable to forge a healthy relationship with my son; the hope that Joe still loved me.

My dad's alarm clock is one of my most important possessions. He hated getting up at 4 a.m. every day and it was his Baby Ben which woke him. It sits on my desk at home. It reminds me of him and the consequences of having no choice about how you live your life when you have no qualifications.

The next lesson I took my father's alarm clock into class – the same despised alarm clock that had rung him out of bed at 4 a.m. every working day – and talked about it as an objective correlative for my relationships with both my father and my son; the whole sense that we can waste time without choosing and once it has passed, it's passed. How I wanted for my son something wonderful, and I felt I'd mucked up the whole thing.

As I said in that original blog, I decided that day that if either son ever asked me to do something I would do it, no matter how much work I had, and I've stuck to that principle fiercely. It's meant me going to bed later, getting up earlier and doing some work stuff *just* well enough. But that's OK – the school's doing fine. Consequently, since that moment in my English class nearly three years ago, my relationship with Joe has, to a great extent, healed.

After a four year gap, the 17-year-old Joe finally had his mates round. They commandeered the front room, played cards to awful music and laughed like we'd wanted them to laugh all those lost years ago when, before Arthur Miller taught me a life lesson, I'd have claimed to have been one of those types who 'always put their family first'.

Tending teachers

> Great teachers know what the conditions for growth are and bad
> ones don't.
>
> Sir Ken Robinson

I would add one more line to Sir Ken's aphorisms: great head teachers know what the conditions for growth are and bad ones don't. Tend teachers if you want them to grow. You need to cultivate an environment which gives your teachers the best possible chance of thriving.

One of the most obvious truisms about schools is that when it comes to educating students, teachers are your greatest resource. Any head teacher who explicitly puts the students first hasn't thought that decision through; the implication is that teachers are less important than students. The best thing for students is a happy, motivated staff; by putting the staff equal first with the students you are doing the best you can do for the students.

It's certainly true that schools do not exist merely to provide teachers with jobs, but if teachers are the most important resource for educating students, you have to tend them, train them and trust them. The trouble is too many head teachers buckle under the pressure of external accountability measures; instead of resisting the climate of fear, they perpetuate it by passing it on down into classrooms where it manifests itself in teaching students to examination hoop-jump. Stephen Plank and Barbara Falk Condliffe found that when it comes to instructional support (i.e. teaching), 'we find classroom quality is lower when classrooms are under greatest pressure to increase test performance.'[2]

No-notice lesson observations, penal performance development systems, mocksteds and general pettiness combine to create a risk-averse classroom culture which eventually stagnates. What we all need

---

[2] Stephen B. Plank and Barbara Falk Condliffe, Pressures of the Season: An Examination of Classroom Quality and High-Stakes Accountability (Baltimore Education Research Consortium, February 2011). Abstract available at: http://aer.sagepub.com/content/50/5/1152.short.

to realise is that head teachers are the single most important defence against the general negativity towards state education. What we have to do is relentlessly exhibit behaviours which are supportive and creative, not penal and reductive. With some irony, we need to behave like we're all in this together.

Professionally I live by Mike Hughes' perceptive aphorism: 'The most effective leaders seem to have erected a sheet of polaroid across the school gate: all the confusing, paradoxical and frustrating initiatives hitting the school, as they pass through the polaroid, emerge as parallel lines, harmonious with *our* plans and processes.'[3] And right now, more than ever, we have to go back to our core values to ensure that the impact upon our schools of chaotic Department for Education policy-making is mitigated.

By shouldering the pressure and keeping your school feeling light and stress-free, your teachers will perform well and the pressure will lift. It is too easy to threaten staff in response to being threatened oneself. Head teachers have to do the opposite. At our school we deliver over 2,000 lessons each week; I cannot teach them all, so I have to develop my colleagues in a safe school environment which allows them to thrive professionally and personally.

Teaching is a demanding job. It is difficult to teach supremely well, lesson after lesson, day after day. If your teachers are not healthy then they will suffer and consequently staff absence will impact upon your students. When expressed like this, it's so obvious that you have to cherish your teachers.

The trouble is most head teachers didn't enter the profession because they were fascinated with employment law. One of the best decisions we made at our school was to employ a qualified human resources manager, Francine Russell. We employ 170 staff; I cannot imagine another organisation of that size operating without an HR manager. The countless benefits of such a post easily outweigh the salary costs. Colleagues have

---

[3]   Mike Hughes, *Tweak to Transform. Improving Teaching: A Practical Handbook for School Leaders* (London: Continuum-3PL, 2002).

immediate expert HR advice available at all times. And watch your short-term sickness rate plummet when you appoint an HR manager – I reckon Francine saves us the equivalent of her salary!

And we need to work to create a sense of unity amongst our colleagues. We have lots of people working in schools but they are divided into teachers and support staff – in the worst schools they are designated as 'non-teaching staff', defined by what they don't do. It's important to do all you can to create the sense of a single staff. Where possible, all policies and practices should apply consistently to teachers and support staff alike.

The 1967 Whitehall Study found that, 'Men in the lowest grade (messengers, doorkeepers, etc.) had a mortality rate three times higher than that of men in the highest grade (administrators)' and concluded that 'more attention should be paid to the social environments, job design, and the consequences of income inequality.'[4] Colleagues who have no autonomy over what they do are the ones who can feel most stressed, whilst head teachers can make choices about nearly every aspect of their working lives.

One of the other problems with head teaching is losing your emotional intelligence. Berne's transactional analysis theory is good for reminding head teachers about how to interact with colleagues.[5] Always work in adult-to-adult mode – the tendency to slip into adult-child mode occurs all too frequently. Develop your emotional intelligence to understand how you must come across to colleagues. And always think about how you would want to be treated.

That said, you won't ever get it all right when it comes to looking after colleagues. All you can do is try your hardest and don't make the same mistake twice! It's not you, it's your designation as head teacher which sometimes makes relationships difficult.

---

[4] See http://en.wikipedia.org/wiki/Whitehall_Study. Whitehall I started in 1967, and Whitehall II in 1984 and is still ongoing. See Whitehall II (also known as the Stress and Health Study) at: http://www.ucl.ac.uk/whitehallII/.

[5] See Eric Berne, *Games People Play: The Psychology of Human Relationship* (London: Penguin, 1973).

If we are about children, we must not forget our own children. I feel very strongly that we shouldn't miss out on the rites of passage moments of our own children just because we are teachers. Implement an extraordinary policy whereby colleagues can take a family day of paid leave which allows them to attend family events or attend to family business. Those colleagues without children might have parents to support or have other important domestic issues to deal with. Our family day policy allowed me to attend my youngest son's Year 6 leavers' assembly – before that I'd missed all of my eldest's most significant moments!

And at the other end of things, it's not until you are a head teacher that you realise the extent to which death impacts upon your colleagues. My very first act as a head teacher was to attend the funeral of a colleague's husband; he'd stayed up to watch TV and she found him dead on the sofa in the morning. No one asks to go to a funeral for fun – you have to grant permission without question.

Similarly, returning from maternity leave is traumatic. It's like a kind of bereavement, so I think you have to be prepared to support new mothers (and fathers) as flexibly as you can. It's difficult to manipulate timetables, but if we are about nurturing young people that should extend to the children of our staff.

None of what is written here means that head teachers should avoid difficult conversations with colleagues who are underperforming. What is important to note, however, is how trust is reciprocal; if you trust your teachers, they will grow to trust you. When you have to make difficult decisions, they will trust you. And they know, anyway, if a colleague isn't performing as well as they might be.

Tending to your staff is a vital element of creating a successful school. As Cheryl Williams, inspired by Dylan Wiliam, so rightly says, 'There is no limit to what we can achieve if we support our teachers in the right way.'[6]

---

[6] Cheryl S. Williams, Building a Strong Teacher Work Force, *Learning First Alliance* (14 August 2013). Available at: http://www.learningfirst.org/building-strong-teacher-work-force.

Much of what I propose is reflected in that model for education advocated by Sir Ken Robinson based on agriculture.[7] The production line is ditched in favour of the organic farm, where the teacher is like the farmer, providing all of the needed ingredients and leaving the crop to grow and thrive. The focus in the agricultural model is on nurturing the learners' talents, as precious and scarce commodities, and on creating the conditions needed for the individual's talents to flourish. Furthermore, in the same way that great teachers grow great students, the SLT has to replicate that process for growing great teachers.

You need to create the conditions for students and staff to reveal their talents and grow through dedicated industry.

So, despite Sir Ken Robinson being out of favour, the language I have used in this book unapologetically reflects our attempt to get the conditions for growth right so that everyone in the school community can thrive as they are inspired to work hard. I use the language of *love* over the language of *fear*.

This much I know about tending your colleagues

- Offer free flu jabs to colleagues – last year nearly half the staff accepted the offer and at £10 a jab it's a bargain, considering a day's cover costs £200+.

- Free tea and coffee facilities in the staffroom aren't too much to ask.

- Set up a well-being committee, and don't micro-manage it. Listen to the feedback and act upon it constructively.

- Send flowers to the parents of new-born babes and to the proper poorly; it's the thought that counts, not the cost.

---

[7] Ken Robinson, How to Escape Education's Death Valley [video], *TED* (10 May 2010). Available at http://www.youtube.com/watch?v=wX78iKhInsc.

● Encourage moments when staff unite in celebration. We finish early on the final day of the autumn term and our chef's team cook us full Christmas lunch. The SLT serves the food to colleagues and we pay for the wine. Secret Santa tops the whole thing off.

The real enemy of promise

Before any great things are accomplished, a memorable change must be made in the system of education ... to raise the lower ranks of society nearer to the higher.

John Adams

Considering our working-class roots it probably seems odd that my dad and I played golf, the most middle class of games. Well, we were not just golfers, we were *artisan* golfers. We were members of the Triangle Artisans, based at the Piltdown Golf Club in East Sussex.

The Oxford English Dictionary defines an artisan as 'a skilled manual worker or craftsman'. Dating back to the 1880s, artisan clubs provided the local working-class men with the opportunity to play golf at the private clubs. They were given a hut in which to change and were restricted to using the course at times when the members of the main club (or parent club) allowed them. In return, the artisans paid a reduced membership fee and helped with the maintenance of the course.

Whilst artisan golf allows the working class to play a game which would otherwise be out of reach, it perpetuates the class divisions within the local community. The parent clubs introduced artisan golf because many of the courses were on common land. Cheap golf was a way of placating the locals. In 1963, when Piltdown Golf Club tried to fence off the course, the greens were sabotaged with weedkiller overnight. They have never tried such a thing again.

My dad was a member of the Triangle Artisans for forty-two years and introduced me to the game when I was 10 years old. At 14, when I was ready to play for the Sussex under 18s, my status as an artisan golfer prohibited me playing for my county. Membership of a full club was required to qualify for representative golf; to have attended a private school was an entry requirement to join Piltdown and so I joined the Crowborough Beacon Golf Club ten miles up the road.

My childhood naivety vanished and I felt the difference between the Triangle's changing hut and the huge country clubhouse across the car park. It was hard to accept the fact that a great golfer would be refused entry to the parent club because he was a bricklayer, yet a retired major-colonel, a privately educated member of the old and silly, with a golf game to match, would be welcomed without question.

So, even in my golfing life, education possessed socioeconomic significance. The fact was, I went to a state comprehensive school; the golfing inequality that engendered was made real every time I had to catch the bus to Crowborough.

It is ironic, then, that in the last 100 years, our country was at its most equal in 1975, the very year I began my secondary school education. In the mid-1970s state school educated Harold Wilson presided over a government which enforced an 83% income tax rate on the super-rich. 83%. Think of that. When I began university in 1984 I received a full grant and tuition fees were unimaginable.

Now, in 2015, I see the impact of the vast divide between rich and poor manifest itself starkly in my job as head teacher of Huntington, the largest school in York. It is a truly comprehensive school. We have the full range of students, from professors' daughters to students from some of the worst socioeconomic backgrounds in the country. Proper poverty.

As the gap between the rich and poor widens I see more students on free school meals, more students whose parents buy second-hand uniforms and more parents who need financial support for school trips. And in the biggest school in York, a wealthy city in the sixth biggest economy in the world, when it rains hard, we put numerous buckets out to catch the water because the roof leaks and we can't afford to repair it.

Even David Cameron knows the corrosive effect of inequality on society. In 2009 he said, 'More unequal countries do worse according to every quality of life indicator.'[1] Yet, in one of the most unequal societies in the developed world, it is tougher than it has ever been for a council house boy like me to make it to the top of the professions. Countries like Finland and Canada, and cities like Shanghai, are striving to establish a meritocracy, to create social cohesion, to provide opportunity for all. And, as our society splinters further, on social and racial and religious grounds, we should be aiming higher too – for all our citizens.

We have to hope. As Billy Bragg once said, 'The enemy of all of us who wish to make the world a better place is not capitalism, not conservatism ... it's our own cynicism ... and we have to fight against our own cynicism.'[2] Cynicism has no place in education. How can working with young people be anything but uplifting?

That said, the last twelve years in education have been incredibly demanding; the politicisation of education has reached unimaginable levels. From the centralist Labour administration with endless key performance indicators which, Soviet-style, had to improve year on year, to the Conservative-led coalition's dismantling of state education, it would have been easy to have given in to our own cynicism.

When we were looking for a school for Joe and Ollie, the clincher for me was the last line in the introduction to St George's RC Primary School's brochure: 'This is a school where love exists.' That was thirteen years ago and in that time the courage to express such sentiments has grown increasingly rare in our pressurised education system.

And the air of menace from the centre hasn't gone away. In her first article for the *Daily Telegraph* after the 2015 Election Nicky Morgan MP, Secretary of State for Education, threatened that *coasting* schools will, euphemistically, 'be given new leadership', because she knows,

---

[1]   David Cameron, annual Hugo Young lecture [video], London, 10 November 2009. Available at: http://www.theguardian.com/commentisfree/2009/nov/11/cameron-hugo-young-progressive-paradox.

[2]   Billy Bragg Talks About Cynicism (21 May 2011). Available at: http://www.youtube.com/watch?v=v4kYsjzuunA.

apparently, that 'works in turning schools around.'[3] I wish I shared her sense of certainty.

What is so hugely heartening, then, is to be growing truly great teaching with colleagues whose moral compass has been unaffected by the movement of the political magnetic poles; colleagues whose priorities have focused unerringly upon doing what is best for the children in their schools; colleagues who have resisted their inner cynicism against the odds and worked for a more equal world; colleagues whose schools continue to be liberated by love not frozen with fear. I have no need to name them – they know who they are.

> And so now I'd like to say – people can change anything they want to. And that means everything in the world. People are running about following their little tracks – I am one of them. But we've all got to stop just following our own little mouse trail. People can do anything – this is something that I'm beginning to learn. People are out there doing bad things to each other. That's because they've been dehumanised. It's time to take the humanity back into the centre of the ring and follow that for a time. Greed, it ain't going anywhere. They should have that in a big billboard across Times Square. Without people you're nothing. That's my spiel.
>
> Joe Strummer[4]

---

[3] Nicky Morgan, We will step up our school reforms so every child can thrive, *Daily Telegraph*, 17 May 2015.

[4] *Joe Strummer: The Future Is Unwritten*, dir. Julien Temple (Vertigo/IFC Films, 2007).

Uckfield Post Office staff, 1955.
Ernest Harry Tomsett (second row, centre)

Select bibliography

Allison, Shaun (2014). *Perfect Teacher-Led CPD* (Carmarthen: Independent Thinking Press).

Barth, Roland S. (1991). *Improving Schools from Within: Teachers, Parents, and Principals Can Make the Difference* (San Francisco, CA: Jossey-Bass).

Barton, Geoff (2014). *Teach Now! The Essentials of Teaching: What You Need to Know to Be a Great Teacher* (London: Routledge).

Bennett, Tom (2013). *Teacher Proof: Why Research In Education Doesn't Always Mean What It Claims, And What You Can Do About It* (London and New York: Routledge).

Berger, Ron (2003). *An Ethic of Excellence: Building a Culture of Craftsmanship With Students* (Portsmouth, NH: Heinemann).

Burkeman, Oliver (2013). *The Antidote: Happiness for People Who Can't Stand Positive Thinking* (Edinburgh: Canongate).

Coles, Tait (2014). *Never Mind the Inspectors* (Carmarthen: Independent Thinking Press).

Collins, Jim (2001). *Good to Great* (London: Random House Business).

Crawford, Donna K., Bodine, Richard J. and Hoglund, Robert G. (1993). *The School for Quality Learning: Managing the School and Classroom the Deming Way* (Champaign, IL: Research Press).

Csikszentmihalyi, Mihaly (2008). *Flow: The Psychology of Happiness* (New York: Harper Perennial Modern Classics).

Doidge, Norman (2007). *The Brain that Changes Itself* (New York, Viking).

Dweck, Carol (2012). *Mindset: The New Psychology of Success* (New York: Robinson).

Elder, Zoë (2012). *Full On Learning* (Carmarthen: Crown House Publishing).

Foer, Joshua (2011). *Moonwalking with Einstein: The Art and Science of Remembering Everything* (New York: Penguin).

Fullan, Michael (2001). *Leading in a Culture of Change* (San Francisco, CA: Jossey-Bass).

Fullan, Michael (2011). *Change Leader: Learning To Do What Matters Most* (San Francisco, CA: Jossey-Bass).

Fullan, Michael (2011). *The Six Secrets of Change: What the Best Leaders Do to Help Their Organizations Survive and Thrive* (San Francisco, CA: Jossey-Bass).

Fullan, Michael and Hargreaves, Andy (2012). *Professional Capital: Transforming Teaching in Every School* (New York: Routledge).

Gawande, Atul (2010). *The Checklist Manifesto: How to Get Things Right* (London: Profile Books).

Gawande, Atul (2014). *Being Mortal: Illness, Medicine and What Matters in the End* (London: Profile Books).

Gladwell, Malcolm (2009). *Outliers: The Story of Success* (London: Penguin).

Goddard, Vic (2014). *The Best Job in the World* (Carmarthen: Independent Thinking Press).

Hattie, John (2011). *Visible Learning for Teachers: Maximizing Impact on Learning* (London: Routledge).

Jones, Rachel (ed) (2014). *Don't Change the Light Bulbs* (Carmarthen: Independent Thinking Press).

Lemov, Doug (2010). *Teach Like a Champion: 49 Techniques That Put Students on the Path to College* (San Francisco, CA: Jossey-Bass).

Lemov, Doug (2012). *Teach Like a Champion Field Guide: A Practical Resource to Make the 49 Techniques Your Own* [inc. DVD] (San Francisco, CA: Jossey-Bass).

Nuthall, Graham (2007). *The Hidden Lives of Learners* (Wellington: New Zealand Council for Educational Research Press).

Palmer, Parker J. (1998). *The Courage to Teach* (San Francisco, CA: Jossey-Bass).

Pink, Daniel (2011). *Drive: The Surprising Truth About What Motivates Us* (New York: Riverhead Books).

Quigley, Alex (2014). *Teach Now! English: Becoming a Great English Teacher* (Abingdon: Routledge).

Robinson, Sir Ken and Aronica, Lou (2009). *The Element* (New York: Penguin).

Robinson, Martin (2014). *Trivium 21c* (Carmarthen: Independent Thinking Press).

Robinson, Viviane (2011). *Student-Centred Leadership* (San Francisco, CA: Jossey-Bass).

Salewicz, Chris (2006). *Redemption Song: The Definitive Biography of Joe Strummer* (London: HarperCollins).

Sherrington, Tom (2014). *Teach Now! Science: The Joy of Teaching Science* (Abingdon: Routledge).

Stobart, Gordon (2014). *The Expert Learner* (Maidenhead: Open University Press).

Syed, Matthew (2011). *Bounce: The Myth of Talent and the Power of Practice* (London: Fourth Estate).

Williams, John (2012 [1965]). *Stoner* (London: Vintage Classics).

Willingham, Daniel T. (2010). *Why Don't Students Like School? A Cognitive Scientist Answers Questions About How the Mind Works and What It Means for the Classroom* (San Francisco, CA: Jossey-Bass).

Willingham, Daniel T. (2012). *When Can You Trust the Experts? How to Tell Good Science from Bad in Education* (San Francisco, CA: Jossey-Bass).